BATTLE OF THE BAND NAMES

THE BEST AND WORST
BAND NAMES EVER

AND ALL THE BRILLIANT, COLORFUL, STUPID ONES IN BETWEEN

BART BULL
DESIGN: DANIELLE YOUNG

Abrams Image
New York

Editor: David Cashion
Designer: Danielle Young
Production Manager: Jacqueline Poirier

Library of Congress Cataloging-in-Publication Data

Bull, Bart.
  Battle of the band names : the best and worst band names ever
and all the brilliant, colorful, stupid ones in between / by Bart Bull.
      p. cm.
  Includes bibliographical references and index.
  ISBN 978-0-8109-9640-3 (alk. paper)
  1. Rock groups—Names. I. Title.

  ML3534.B853 2009
  781.6601'4—dc22
  2008033849

Printed and bound in China
10 9 8 7 6 5 4 3 2 1

Abrams Image books are available at special discounts when purchased in
quantity for premiums and promotions as well as fundraising or educational
use. Special editions can also be created to specification. For details, contact
specialmarkets@hnabooks.com or the address below.

HNA
harry n. abrams, inc.
a subsidiary of La Martinière Groupe

115 West 18th Street
New York, NY 10011
www.hnabooks.com

TABLE OF CONTENTS

Introduction

Q: Why do you call the band the Mysterians?

A: When we first started, we'd play a show, and the announcer would say, "Well, what's your name?" And I'd say, "We're just a group, we don't have a name." They'd say, "We have to announce something," so I'd make one up, and after that night, we'd drop it right away. We were always the nameless group and I wanted to keep it that way, but it's hard to do.

— ? (Singer/songwriter/frontman/visionary of ? and the Mysterians) from an interview in the Memphis Commercial Appeal

Hold it—let's start all over again. Let's get real, real gone for a change.

Let's go deep into the 1950s—let's journey back to 1954, back to the birth of probably the greatest white rock 'n' roll band of their day, the Rolling Stones. You've heard of 'em, right?

There they are, five wild-eyed white boys way down deep in the Delta, rockin' out at Mississippi State frat-house parties and then heading off to record at Sun Studios. Which was perfectly natural, since the Rolling Stones had bought their very first guitars at O.K. Houck Music Company on Union Avenue in Memphis, right down the street from Sun Studios. Well, sir, the Rolling Stones story is a long one, and a typical one in a lot of ways, but let it be said that they covered themselves in glory, these white boys inspired by the blues. And eventually, as all bands do, as all bands inevitably must, they broke up. (It was due to musical differences.) And from the ashes of the Rolling Stones came another band, with another name, and on that fresh new name hung all hope: the Dawnbreakers.

You've probably never even heard of the Dawnbreakers, have you? Or not even their hot single, "Tough, Tough, Tough," backed with "Give Me a Lock of Yo' Curly Hair," by Andy Anderson and the Dawnbreakers on the Century Limited label out of Jackson, Mississippi, in May 1960, back when wee Keith Richards and li'l Micky Jagger were begging their poor beleaguered British mums for spare shillings so they could nip off a postal order to the States to Chess Records in Chicago, Illinois, and arrange to have them post a copy of the latest long-playing phonograph album from the delightfully named Muddy Waters or Howlin' Wolf. Ah, but inevitably the Dawnbreakers broke up too, despite the fact that they'd gotten even bigger than the Rolling Stones had, and Andy Anderson—born on a plantation in Clarksdale, Mississippi—returned to the electrical supply business. And then Andy got caught up in the Hollywood actor business, and then the rock band management business, and then—it was the seventies already—starting a new band of his own named The Eagle and the Hawk and creating a new label called Aerie and then falling into the real estate business in Taos, New Mexico, and then creating a construction firm in Kentucky, and then recording in Nashville and then at Malaco in Jackson, Mississippi, and then at Criterion in Miami, and by this time there was another band named the Rolling Stones . . . and well, surely you know all the rest from there.

Because a band name is a band's fortune and fame, right? Am I right? Or OK, maybe I'm not right—but if not, even so, it definitely feels like that when the drummer is refusing to mess up his new drumhead by painting "The Silver Beetles" on it in gold stencil lettering. And just because he and his cousin who isn't even in the band both think that "Destiny Fayte" is a way cooler name. Which is to say that while the name of the band may not entirely determine the fateful destiny of the band, it can definitely, massively, profoundly fuck it up. And sadly, every so often, the drummer and his dipstick cousin are right.

OK, so let's establish some rules here when naming your band: there are none. But there are all kinds of rules when it comes to being in a band:

There are no beers at rehearsal, or at least left where your little brother can see 'em so he can rat you out to your dad, and then we won't be able to practice at my house anymore.

And no girlfriends at rehearsals (unless we're talking about Jessica, who is ridiculously babe-bodacious and thus inspirational for songwriting purposes).

No rehearsing drum solos at rehearsals. (In fact, we've been meaning to schedule a band meeting to talk about the whole drum solo thing. We kind of want to cut it out of the set. We only did it that one time because we all drank too much beer back-stage and we needed to hit the can in the middle of the set, so a drum solo made a lot of sense. But it's kind of killing our momentum. And we really need our momentum. A lot more than we need another drum solo. Sorry, dude. Don't take it personally.)

And this one's An Absolute Rule: Never Let Your Mom Take Your Band Photo! Never! Ever! I don't care if she's a professional photographer and takes band photos for a living! I don't care if she's Annie Leibovitz! Or Roberta Bayley, who took the cover photo for the very first Ramones album! I don't care if she's Pam Springsteen! (Especially her, actually.) Never Ever Let The Mother Of Anybody In The Band Take The Band Photo! Just Say No! At worst, have her hand the camera to your dad and have her show him which button to push. If your dad takes it, the band will be all defensive because he's already pretty much let everybody know that he thinks they're all geeks and feebs who steal his beer and don't have jobs and never play any of the great songs he suggests, and thus the resulting photos will reflect aggression and paranoia and stuff. If your mom takes it, you're all going to look like little fluffy bunnies wearing bunny pajamas with bunny feet and bunny ears, no matter how fierce and desperate you try to look.

But here's a rule that isn't so obvious: a band begins not at the first rehearsal, or the first gig, but when they first decide on a name. Which often comes before the first rehearsal, and often comes long after the first gig.

Some Band Naming Rules: (Forget what I said over there somewhere— of course there's rules. What do you think this is? Like, total anarchy, dude? I don't think so—why else would you be ready to sign a 173-page major label contract, offering them breakage deductions, and all publishing and merchandise ownership—should anyone ever ask you to—which they won't, of course . . . but they might . . . it could happen.

During certain decades, names that spell the same frontward and backward are considered super-cool—or SupeR-CooL—because you can make amazing logos out of them. During those same decades, if your name doesn't do that, you can cut out your logo and put a mirror underneath and kind of achieve the same effect. Now that there's Photoshop, you don't have to take a picture and then sort of trace around it, which generally means you get better results. Generally.

This one's not a rule, it's just common sense: don't use "electric" in your name, like the Electric Prunes, or the Electric Flag, or the Electric Indian, or the Electric Elves, or even the Electric Eels. Or "flying," like the Flying Burrito Brothers, or the Flying Circus, or the Flying Machine. Not unless you were actually in one of those bands during the late 1960s. Because by the time 1969 became 1970, they already sounded incredibly corny. And then you've got to start calling yourselves the Burrito Brothers, or the Machine, or Elf.

And another thing . . . and this one's gonna take a while, so you may want to sit down and, well, kind of shut up. I'm gonna be very, very helpful to you here, kind of like your Uncle Larry. Except not like your Uncle Larry at all. Because, well, you know your Uncle Larry? And you know how he's like one of your biggest fans and supporters and stuff? And you know how after he saw you play like your very second gig of all time, he invited you over to his basement the very next Tuesday? And once he got everybody over there, he opened up his custom-built cabinets and revealed his own personal collection of guitars from back when he used to be in bands? And the bands were mostly named Shattered Crucifixz until he and the lead singer got born again and so they regrouped and renamed the band Battered Crucyfixz? And so he made this big announcement to you and your whole band that because he was so inspired by your gig and all, that you could each pick out one of his amazing collection of guitars to use at your next gig? And all of his guitars were like in the shape of skulls with serpents crawling out of the eyeholes, or they were serpents with skulls crawling out of their eyeholes, or something like that. Or had Jesus on them. And for a post-alternative, post-emo band with the name We're Not In So Great Of A Mood Right Now, it would have kind of looked . . . well, you know. You know?

OK, so here's my point: eventually, in like about ten minutes or so, you and most of your band are going to pretty much look a whole lot like your fat-ass Uncle Larry. Jimmy's asymmetrical emo comb-over is starting to look just like a regular, plain-old comb-over because he's going bald faster than global warming. And well, guess what. It's like totally contagious, and pretty soon, you're all going to be fat, and old, and stupid, and lame, and horrible. And bald. And the chances are very high that your band name is going to sound even dopier, a decade or so from now, than the Gaynotes, or the Ultimate Spinach, or Shrieking Valkyrie, or Adolf Hofner and the Oklahoma Playboys. The half-life of a band name can make the cheapest drugstore chocolate Easter bunny look like it's hanging tough like Stonehenge. So choose wisely, Grasshopper. Choose ever so wisely.

There is A Certain Ratio (let's call it "A Certain Ratio"), between the fame and success and album sales and ticket sales and chick-magnetism and logo-nosity of a name, but the problem is all of that comes clean only after you hear it rattling around in the clothes-dryer spin cycle.

Like, for instance, Pink Floyd. I'm sorry, but that's a dumb-ass name. Nobody's ever going to go see a band like that. OK, it's good in some ways, because it's got only two syllables and they're pretty hard to misspell but still. Consider something else, something a little snappier.

Or another example: U2. I mean, you've got to ask yourself whether anybody down at the local newspaper in Dublin is ever going to manage to spell the thing right for your regular Tuesday night gig at the pub, or if you actually convince the pub to put an ad in the paper when you finally work your way up to Saturday night, if they're not going to spell it "You Two." Or "You Too." Or "Yootoo." Or worse.

But then once you actually get to be Pink Floyd or U2 or the Beatles or the Rolling Stones or Talking Heads (well, not them, because no one ever got that one right no matter how famous they became, even after they grumpily called one of their albums *The Name of This Band Is Talking Heads*) well, once you're a massive huge internationally successful mega-band, nobody even cares anymore that you came from Australia and never really understood that calling yourself AC/DC might well suggest that you were bisexual or something. Or that nobody can figure out whether you pronounce Live like "live" or like "live." And it's all because of "A Certain Ratio."

But you have to remember that it's called "A Certain Ratio" because . . . it's a ratio. Because otherwise, it would mean that The Greatest Band Names In The History Of The World, as based on just album sales, pretty much, would be the BeeGees and the Eagles and Fleetwood Mac and the Beatles and Michael Jackson and so forth. And while those are all pretty OK band names, one and all, it's hard to say they're like The Best Band Names Ever because then probably the Eighth Best Band Name Ever would be Celine Dion, and we'd all know then for certain that the Book of Revelations was kicking full effect. But once again, it's "A Certain Ratio" swooping in to save us from the Scary Apocalyptic Beast Of The Endless French-Canadian Multiple-Cowriter Power-Ballad.

It's "A Certain Ratio" means that a band name like My Bloody Valentine, which seems totally rad and perfect to its audience, also kind of creeps out the Celine Dion crowd, which also seems really rad and perfect.

Once you're a giant success, of course, "A Certain Ratio" means that you can pretty much sell a lot of T-shirts with whatever you put on there on them. Like the Grateful Dead, who sold—or, OK, to be accurate, usually it was some crusty trustafarian in the parking lot who actually sold 'em—shirts with skulls (can't go wrong with those, ever) and roses (always have some merch for the ladies, definitely) and dancing teddy bears (uhm, well, it can't hurt if your audience is also tripping their brains out).

Meanwhile, let us pause for a moment and briefly consider the thin line between genius, insanity, and semi-genius, and consider what exactly makes a great band name great and what makes a bad name so astonishingly-boneheadedly-numbnutsingly-transcendently-transcendentally awful.

First of all, let's talk about spelling. Because the drummer has to write it on the head of his Kick drum and we all know that if Dennis gets a chance to screw it up, he's gonna Screw It Up Royale. And then there's the fact that if you ever actually get a gig, and that gig gets listed in the free listings of the local free paper, or even better but worse, in the ads for the club, the club owner is going to screw it up when he sends it in.

So spelling is important. And thus, one of the most important questions that most bands will ever have to consider: two X's or three? And the answer is, unquestionably and universally, three. If only because then it also looks like the old-fashioned symbol for whiskey, and hey, how could that hurt?

Consider such issues as pronunciation: take a name like "The Surfires." Did they really want to be known, as they undoubtedly were, as the Surf Ires, or the Surf Irees, or the Sir Fires? Because pronouncing it as "The Shure Fires" would look to be like Option Numero Ocho or so.

And take a name like "Teddy and the Bears." Ouch. Just because your name is Teddy, or Ted, or Theodore, or Beaver F. Cleaver doesn't mean you should let it determine the name of your band. This is a truly tragic tale, because as it happens, Teddy and the Bears had the songs, the chops, the style, and the nerve to go all the way and become one of the fiercest success stories in the whole history of death-Emocore but then they made a tragic band name mistake, and the whole thing began to unravel. Take a lesson from Teddy and from the Bears.

And we live in the era of the Internet, the Web, the search engine, so if you name your band the Gettysburg Address; or Wuthering Heights; or Subway Sandwiches; or the Grapes of Wrath; or The Bureau of Alcohol, Tobacco and Firearms (although that last one is actually kind of cool) you're going to end up kind of low on the list.

Take your time and ponder each and every name that follows. There's a great lesson to be learned in every great band name and from every bad band name, and often even more than one lesson— like "Why did they decide they absolutely had to capitalize the 'a' in 'and' but not the 't' in 'the'?"

In the end, to be included in this book, a band name had to have appeared on a big hit record, or a flop record, or a record that never made it big enough to flop. But a record, anyway. Or a CD, or a cassette, or an MP3, or an eight-track—no exceptions. Or else the band name had to appear on a poster, or a flyer, or be written with a Sharpie marker in a gnarly-ass club dressing room, or be the only one on a list of like twenty-five different names that didn't get totally scratched out when those fuckin' little hardcore twerps came through with their spray paint. Or you had to have a MySpace site— OK, so I realize that means that it's kind of wide open, but what can you do? I mean some of the bands on MySpace are listenable. Well, I heard one, this one time, that didn't totally suck.

A Small Smattering from among the Top 10,000 Worst Band Names Ever

Uh, dude, I realize that you've spent a lot of years all alone in your bedroom practicing and . . . well, doing other stuff, and it has sort of left you a little confused, a tad bit out of touch with reality, or at least with the kind of reality that's outside your bedroom. Because why else would you have named your band Kajagoogoo? Or Archers of Loaf? Or Renaissance Carwash?

Beneath the names assembled below like tombstones in handy rows—read 'em and weep—lie the shattered dreams of many lost souls, musicians, and drummers alike, listlessly wandering the corridors of what's left of their own ambitions, doomed to wonder eternally if the reason they never really made it big was because they agreed to call their band Yellow Stain. Or if the record would have sold if they hadn't let the record label change their name from the K-Otics to Sodom and Gamera. Or trying to remember just which band member came up with the Proctors. At night sometimes, if you listen closely, you can hear their anguished howls, lonely and piercing, like banshees, like coyotes, like Geddy Lee: *"I told them Sister Mary Bob was a stupid name!"*

The Clergymen

The Lemon Pipers

Captain Beyond

The Blues Magoos

The Poquellos

Jack B. Nimble and the Quicks

The Jury

The Stoics

Wham!

Les Chausettes Noire

The Grateful Dead

Milton Brown and His
Musical Brownies

The Prisonaires

The Tokens

Bachman-Turner Overdrive

Crosby, Stills, Nash, & Young
with Reeves and Taylor

Lipps Inc.

*NSYNC

Ace Bailey and His
Utah Trailers

Sigue Sigue Sputnik

Archers of Loaf

Dewayne and the Beldettas

Buddy and Bob

The Genitorturers

Pablo Cruise

Haircut 100

Eveleyn Dell and the
Vibratones

Thunder

Pink Cream 69

Styx

Skinny Puppy

Oingo Boingo (formerly The
Mystic Knights of Oingo Boingo)

The Rollins Band

The Swingin' Medallions

Korn

Professor Longhair
and His Blues Scholars

Limp Bizkit

Phish

The Flower Pot Men

Tribute

The Folk Girls

Cap'n Jazz

Business Card

The Ultimate Spinach

John Cafferty and the
Beaver Brown Band

The Namelosers

Crashdiet

Happy Fats Leblanc and
the Rayne-Bo Ramblers

P. J. Orion and The Magnates

Al & His Pals

Aswad

Vom

The Commodores

Betty Amos and The
Lump Boys

The Tempo-Tones

Elston Gunn and His Rock
Boppers (later, Bob Dylan)

The White Bucks

Atomic Rooster

The Von Trapp Family Singers

The Supermen Lovers

The Music Explosion

The Archies

The Charlatans UK

KC & the Sunshine Band

Mel Taylor & The Dynamics

Nation of Ulysses

The Marigolds

Binky Jones and
the Americans

The Hippy's

The Tunedrops

Barbarian Wrath

Menswear

The Golliwogs

Adolph Hofner and The
Pearl Wranglers (formerly
Adolph Hofner and All The
Boys, Adolph Hofner and the
San Antonians, Adolph Hofner
and His Texans, The Hawaiian
Serenaders, Adolph Hofner
and the Oklahoma Playboys)

Wang Chung

Stryper

The Silver Jews

It's a Beautiful Day

Children of the Mushroom

The Zoofs

The Neon Lighted People

Scotlinde Yarde

Webb Pierce and the Wondering Boys

The Blue Beatles

The Greek Fountains

The Baytovens

William Penn and His Pals

The Fe-Fi-Four Plus Two

Klymaxx

The Lollipop Shoppe

Zolar X

The Balladeers

Uncle Rufe Armstrong and His Coon Hunters

Celtic Frost

Dr. Zoom and the Sonic Boom (previously Ocean, later Bruce Springsteen and the E Street Band)

Pud (later The Doobie Brothers)

Mother Mallard's Portable Masterpiece Company

The Liver Birds

The Electric Flag

The French Church

The Cyril Lords

Diabolical Masquerade

Cinderella

The Linc-Tones (later The Tokens, meaning they actually chose not merely one but two of the worst band names ever)

John and Gunther

Healing Force

The Fabulous Rhythm Makers

The Harmonicos

The Hi-Guys

Savatage

Prefab Sprout

Lady Windemere's Operation

The Werps

All-Saved Freak Band

Fotheringay

Mike Mann and The Men

Captain Matchbox Whoopee Band

Flash and the Inmates

Fink-Muncx IX

Freddie and the Swinging Batchelors

Country Radio

Kix

The Fabulous Chancellors

The Fabulous Morticians

The Klanzmen

The Serendipity Singers

The Che-Vals

The Pentatones

Yama and the Karma Dusters

Le Max

Exciter

Boy Blue and The Moon

The Phi-Dels

Texas Is The Reason

The Regents (previously Tacoma The Crisis)

Let's Active

The Lubocs

Sunshine (formerly Liquid Sunshine)

Sparky & the Starfires

The Swags

Fyre

Mickey and the Clean Cuts

Hobo Hank and The Sons of the DeltaSecret Oyster

Murple

The String Cheese Incident

The Green Fuz (with one z)

Jerry & the Jerrimen

The Metro-Nomes

Softrock

The Pied Pipers

The Frazz

Gandharva Rock and Show Band (Highlight: Our Hammond organ was previously owned by Paul Revere and the Raiders)

Ian Saxon and the Creditors

The Landlords

Tsutsumi Hiroshi and All Stars Wagon

The Vandaliers

The Alarm Clocks

Behold the Arctopus

The Intimate Blues Connection

Th' Dudes

The Heck

THE CALL

THE TOLL

THE BEAU DENTURIES

THE SURFIRES

FREEDOM EXPRESS

CHRIS AND CRAIG

FOURMYULA

THE TYGERS OF PANG TANG

1910 FRUITGUM COMPANY

THE FIXX

RICHARD PASH AND THE BACKDOOR SOCIETY

NU SHOOZ

BLU SHOEZ

SHOES

KAL-Q-LATED RISK

LARRY AND THE LADDERS

THE FERRARIS OF CANADA

CRYPTIC SLAUGHTER

TONY AND THE INITIALS

A MYTHICAL MEADOW

THE BRITISH MODBEATS

DYSRHYTHMIA

THE COMIN' GENERATION

RETURN TO FOREVER

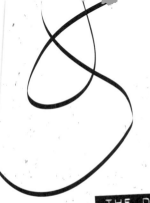

THE DEAD MILKMEN

KAK

BIOFEEDBACK

ALL SPORTS BAND

JEFF AND PENNY

DEEP TURTLE

THE HOTSY TOTSY BOYS (LATER
LAWRENCE WELK'S HONOLULU
FRUIT GUM ORCHESTRA, LATER
LAWRENCE WELK AND HIS
CHAMPAGNE MUSIC MAKERS)

STORMTROOPERS OF DEATH

ENUFF Z'NUFF

THE GETTYSBURG ADDRESS

THE RITES OF SPRING

JUSTIN TYME

THE KREW KUTS

THE DECRESCENDOS

LOVERBOY

The Munn Singers

The Denems

The Sugar Shoppe

Pist.On

Dragonwyck

The Binary Marketing Show

Johnny Winter And
The Del-Rhythmettes

Michel and the French
Canadians

Crazy Lixx

Red & Les Trio

Idaho

The Vinnie Vincent Invasion

Tuff

The Electric Prunes

Kajagoogoo

Mouse & the Traps

Sergio Mendes & Brazil '66

Rebecca and the
Sunnybrook Farmers

United Empire Loyalists
(formerly The Molesters)

Cranberry Moustache

Toto

Madgic

Jimmy Rabbitt and the Karats

The Reekers (later The Hangmen,
then, sadly, The Button)

Lorraine and the Socialites

Zao

The Black Noodle Project

The Hondells

Virgin Steele

The Archies

Lonesome George and the
Eubanks Brothers

Louie & The Leprechauns

Larry Lee and the Leesures

Inflatable Boy Clams

The Go

The Do

The Grapes of Wrath

Flux of Pink Indians

Unearth

Jejune

The German Bonds

Champaign

The Liver Birds

A Flock of Seagulls

The Gay Lads

Clap Your Hands Say Yeah

Black Bolt and the
Silver Ferns

Capell Hopkins Blues Dredge

The New Haven Women's
Liberation Rock Band

The Cardigans

The Doodletown Pipers

The Implicit

Piece Kor

The Turfits

The Fabulous Plaids

The Chaen Reaction

The Unknown IV

The Calvary-Aires

The Threads of Fybre

a-ha

The Intercoms

The Weird Street Carnival

The More-Tishans

Moby Dick and the Whalers

The Mustard Men

The Hello People

Winger

Color Me Badd

The Dynamic Dial-Tones

The Groop

Eyes and Arms of Smoke

The Five Blobs

Cosmic Brotherhood

Tony Ashley and the Delicates

The Dinks

Gary Mac and the Mac Truques

Pere Ubu

The Peppermint Rainbow

Spider and the Crabs

Upside Dawne

Hüsker Dü

Oasis

Dance of the Branch

The Folklords

Van Der Graaf Generator

Underground Sunshine

Two Cats and a Kitten

The Torne Payges

The Beavers

Further Seems Forever

The Cliches

The Fabulous Depressions

Egyptian Candy

Drive Like Jehu

The Epicureans

Wu-Tang Clan

Lothar and the Hand People

The Friedles

The United States of America

The Presidents of the United
States of America

Orchestral Manoeuvres
In The Dark (later OMD)

The Proverbial Knee Hi's

The Rhythm Checkers

The Revolting Cocks

Surgical Penis Klinik

Tomorrow (previously
The In Crowd, later Four Plus
One [hat trick!])

The Open Mind

The Nashville Teens

Fury

Britny Fox

New Fast Automatic
Daffodils

Handsome Boy
Modeling School

Ned's Atomic Dustbin

The Mars Volta

Little Feat

&
and
&

The fierce & damnable dilemma of being in any band that includes **"and"** in the name is The Curse Of The Dreaded Ampersand. (Or not, depending if you and your band—You **&** The Other Guys—are doing this in one of those rare demi-decades when The Ampersand seems groovy.) (From early 1978, in other words, to midsummer 1981.) (Or else it just helps the name fit on the bass drumhead.) Because it's almost a dead certain guarantee that if you decide that you're You **And** The Other Guys, everybody who ever prints a flyer or puts a listing in the newspaper is going to go all fancy on you and use an ampersand. And there's only one way to get around it, for all practical purposes. You're just going to have to boil the name down to The Other Guys. And then start debating about whether you need one Z or two.

Don & Juan

Paul & Paula

Shirley & Lee

Mickey & Sylvia

Santo & Johnny

Skip & Flip

Jan & Dean

Stan & Dean

Sam and Dave

Peter and Gordon

Chad and Jeremy

Sonny & Cher
(originally Caesar and Cleo, later,
Cher, then Congressman Bono)

Ian & Sylvia

Pepsi & Shirlie

Salt -N- Pepa

The Mamas & The Papas (formerly
The Mugwumps, The Big Three, The Journeymen)

Simon & Garfunkel
(formerly Tom And Jerry)

Zager & Evans

Brewer and Shipley

Loggins & Messina

Ike and Tina Turner & The Ikettes

The Captain & Tennille

England Dan and John Ford Coley

Tony Orlando & Dawn

Peaches & Herb

Mel & Tim

Mel & Kim

Hall & Oates

Wendy and Lisa

Crosby, Stills & Nash

Crosby, Stills, Nash, & Young

Crosby Stills, Nash, & Young with
Taylor and Reeves

The Stills-Young Band

CSN

Souther, Hillman, & Furay

Emerson, Lake, and Palmer

Beck, Bogert, and Appice

Blood Sweat & Tears

Dave Dee, Dozy, Beaky, Mick & Titch

Hamilton, Joe Frank, & Reynolds

B. Bumble and the Stingers

Jack B. Nimble and the Quicks

Frankie Lyman and the Teenagers

Lewis Lymon and the Teen Chords

Barry Darvell and the Blazers

Dyke and The Blazers

Gary Glitter and the Glitter Band

David Bowie and the Spiders From Mars
(formerly Davie Jones and the King Bees, then the
Manish Boys, Davie Jones and the Lower Third,
and David Bowie and the Buzz)

David Peel and the Lower East Side

Jimmy Gilmer and the Fireballs

Buddy Holly and The Crickets

Maurice Williams and the Zodiacs (formerly the Royal
Charms, then the Gladiolas, then the Excellos, then merely The Zodiacs)

Archie Bell & the Drells

Curtis Mayfield and the Impressions
(also Jerry Butler and the Impressions,
and The Impressions)

Brenda and the Tabulations

Brenda and the Big Boys

Brenda and the Big Dudes

Rosie and The Originals

Vince Vance and the Valiants

Stark Naked and the Car Thieves

Dr. Hook and The Medicine Show

Spanky and Our Gang

Kool & the Gang

George Clinton and the P-Funk All-Stars
(previously Parliament-Funkadelic,
previously The Parliaments)

Junior Walker and the All Stars
(formerly the Jumping Jacks)

Little Walter and the Aces

Desmond Dekker and the Aces

The Rhythm Aces

Preston Jackson and the Rhythm Aces

Jabbo Smith's Rhythm Aces

The Amazing Rhythm Aces

Ace

Cathy Jean and the Roommates

Ruby and the Romantics

Louis Jordan and His Tympany Five

Nellie Lutcher and Her Rhythm

Julia Lee and Her Boyfriends

Joe Turner and His Blues Kings

Joe Liggins and His Honeydrippers

Roy Milton and His Solid Senders

Paul Williams and His Hucklebuckers

Stick McGhee and His Buddies

Jacki Brenston with His Delta Cats

Jimmy Liggins and His 3-D Music

LaVern Baker and The Gliders

Clyde McPhatter and the Drifters

Billy Ward and the Dominoes

Thurston Harris and the Sharps

Jimmy James and the Blue Flames
(later the Jimi Hendrix Experience)

Randy and the Rainbows

Donny and Marie

Pink Lady and Jeff

...And You Will Know Us by the Trail of Dead

I don't know whether you've noticed this, but when you look on the flyer, everybody else's band name looks totally stupid, and yours is really amazing. Well, if not amazing, at least it's not totally stupid. Or if not totally stupid, only somewhat stupid. If everybody else's is totally stupid, at least you're only about the thirtieth band in the history of rock 'n' roll to decide that if you call yourself Free Beer, you'll always get good positioning on the poster. It was either that, or call yourself one of these names, and these were already taken. Although you could say the same thing about Free Beer, only more so.

The Mr. T Experience

Dread Zeppelin

Deep Turtle

JON COUGAR CONCENTRATION CAMP

Squid Vicious

New Squids on the Dock

The Traveling Dingleberries

The New Crusty Nostrils

Black Shit Puppy Farm

Anus The Menace

Butthole Surfers

Fudge Tunnel

Eve's Plum

Trulio Disgracios

The DayGlo Abortions

Los Mex Pistols Del Norte

Sandy Duncan's Eye

Vic Morrow's Head

Jody Foster's Army

Dead Kennedys

The Dead Milkmen

The Grateful Dead

Nerf Herder

Penis Flytrap

Anal Cunt

The Queers

1000 Homo DJs

Gaye Bikers On Acid

The Pink Fairies

Stark Naked and the Car Thieves

Buck Naked and the Bare Bottom Boys

Buck Satan and the 666 Shooters

Adolf Satan

Root Boy Slim and the Sex-Change Band with the Rootettes

Sam The Sham and the Pharoahs

The Falling Wallendas

The Zambonis

The Zoofs

The Peanut Butter Conspiracy

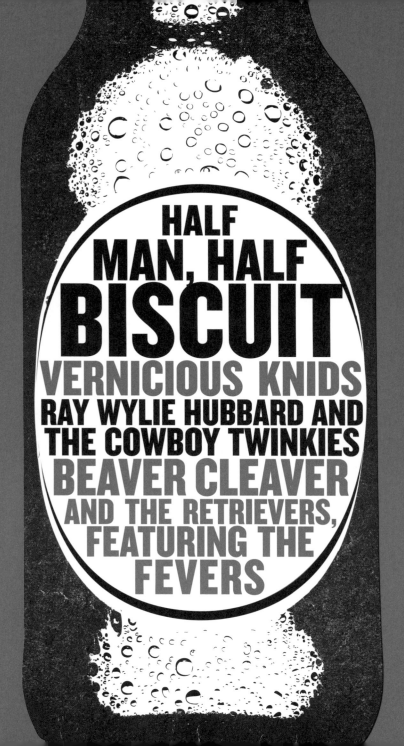

HALF MAN, HALF BISCUIT
VERNICIOUS KNIDS
RAY WYLIE HUBBARD AND THE COWBOY TWINKIES
BEAVER CLEAVER AND THE RETRIEVERS, FEATURING THE FEVERS

Don't Eat the Brown Acid, a Lighter Shade of Pale, or the Dreadful Grape

Take a moment, kids, and consider. Or if not, at least think about it like this: And We Will Know You By The Trail Of Dead Band Name Adjectives And Articles. And Adverbs. Because I don't know whether you want to believe me about this or not, but there was a time when bands like the Jefferson Airplane, and Quicksilver Messenger Service, and Creedence Clearwater Revival, and the Grateful Dead were, like, really big famous bands that everybody had heard of and knew about and stuff. And the more people knew about 'em, the more they were inclined to ditch most of the clanking loose parts that were rattling around under the hoods of their band names and just call 'em the Airplane, and Quicksilver, and Creedence, and the Dead. Because there you are, hanging around Woodstock, or Altamont, or the Fillmore East, or West, or any of those places that hippies congregate. And while you're having a great time and all, everybody knows that the Summer of Love isn't going to last all summer. And soon enough, it's time to bust a move, slap on a tie and maybe some shoes, and go sell out quick. If only so you can afford to buy tickets to shows from one of the many Grateful Dead offshoots, tickets that have gotten awfully pricey of late, especially when you add in service charges, and parking, and babysitting, and all. Well, all this takes time, precious time, valuable time, time that can't be wasted by constantly pronouncing every single syllable in Quicksilver Messenger Service. Which wouldn't fit on the ticket anyway, not with today's prices on there too . . . So consider brevity, kids, as a form of poetry, as well. Time waits for no man. Oh, and make sure they can read your name on the poster. Psychedelic lettering is really far out and all, but then, nobody has actually spoken the phrase "far out" in three decades without being in a movie about hippies on a bus, or a commune, or somewhere. So, like, consider, you know?

The Jefferson Airplane (*formerly of The Town Criers; The Great Society; then Jefferson Starship, then Starship, then Jefferson Starship—The Next Generation; also Hot Tuna; Bodacious; Bodacious D.F.; SVT; KBC Band; Moby Grape; and others*)

The Seeds, or Sky Saxon and the Seeds (*formerly Richie Marsh and the Hood, later, Sky Saxon and the Electra Fires, Sky Saxon and the Soul Rockers, Sky Saxon Blues Band, Sky Sunlight and the World Peace Band, Stars New Seeds, Sky Sunlight Saxon and the Original Seeds, Sky Sunlight Saxon's Dragonslayers, Sky Sunlight Saxon's U.S.A.*)

Quicksilver Messenger Service (*later Quicksilver, then the Dinosaurs*)

Big Brother and the Holding Company (*formerly Blue Yard Hill, later The Kozmic Blues Band*)

The Doors (*formerly Rick and The Ravens; The Psychedelic Rangers; later The Doors of the 21st Century, then The Resurrection of the Doors[litigation]*)

The Jimi Hendrix Experience (*formerly of The Casuals; The King Casuals; Bobby Taylor and the Vancouvers; The Imperials; The Rainflowers; Jimmy James and the Blue Flames; later The Electric Sky Church; Gypsy, Sun, and Rainbows; The Band of Gypsys; Gypsy Sun Moon and Stars; and others*)

Love

The Electric Flag

Harpers Bizarre

Beacon Street Union

The Chocolate Watch Band (*formerly The Hogs*)

Strawberry Alarm Clock

The Electric Prunes

Moby Grape

The Magick Powerhouse of Oz (*previously The Orkustra, later the Freedom Orchestra [of San Quentin Prison] Featuring Bobby Beausoleil [formerly of the Manson Family]*)

The Milky Way (*featuring Charles Manson*)

The Ultimate Spinach

The Daily Flash

Bubble Puppy

Shiva's Head Band

The Peanut Butter Conspiracy

Cat Mother and the All Night Newsboys

Frumious Bandersnatch

It's a Beautiful Day

The Loading Zone

Lothar and the Hand People

The Moving Sidewalks

Gentle Reign

The Flat Earth Society

Mother Load

The Ace of Cupsa

Mother Earth

Salvation Army Banned

Commodore Condello's Salt River Navy Band

The Blues Magoos

The Moody Blues

The Blues Image

The Golden Dawn

H. P. Lovecraft

The Music Emporium

Savage Resurrection

Mouse and the Traps

Bloodrock

Autosalvage

Sly and the Family Stone

Tonto's Expanding Headband

Mother Mallard's Portable Masterpiece Company

Nirvana (*from the UK*)

The Red Crayola

The Silver Apples

The Soft Machine

The Sons of Champlin

Sopwith Camel

The West Coast Pop Art Experimental Band
(*formerly The AlleyKats, The Snowmen, The Rogues*)

The United States of America

Kaleidoscope

Cream (*later Blind Faith; Ginger Baker's Air Force; Baker-Gurvitz Army; West, Bruce, And Laing; Derek and The Dominoes; and others*)

Iron Butterfly
*(later Iron Butterfly With
Pinera and Rhino)*

Golden Earring
(formerly The Earrings)

Led Zeppelin
*(formerly The
New Yardbirds)*

Vanilla Fudge
*(originally The Electric Pigeons;
then The Pigeons; later Cactus;
then Beck, Bogert, and Appice)*

Steppenwolf
*(formerly The Sparrows,
The Sparrow, Sparrow)*

Pink Floyd

Blue Cheer

Black Sabbath

Deep Purple

Clear Light

Tangerine Dream

Jethro Tull

Uriah Heep

Ten Years After

Humble Pie

Atomic Rooster

Grand Funk Railroad

Buffalo Springfield

Candied Egg Plant

The Holy Modal Rounders

The New Tweedy Brothers

Winter's Green

The Fifth Dimension

The Five Day Week Straw People

United Empire Loyalists *(formerly The Molesters)*

Black Zephyr Orchestra

The Dream Syndicate

Mother's Own Electrified Fuzz Band

The MysteryTrend

Alexander's Timeless Bloozband

Aphrodite's Child

Bangor Flying Circus

The Crazy World of Arthur Brown

The Captain Matchbox Whoopee Band

Chocolate Watch Band

Circus Maximus

Dr. West's Medicine Show and Junk Band

The Druids of Stonehenge

Earth Opera

Frijid Pink

Elmer Gantry's Velvet Opera

Great Metropolitan Steam Band

Haphash and The Colored Coat

The Hello People

The Human Beinz

The Illusion

The Lemon Pipers

The Love Generation

The Mandrake Memorial

The Moving Sidewalks

Perth County Conspiracy

Red Krayola

The Sapphire Thinkers

Shiva's Headband

The Shocking Blue

The World of Oz

The Yellow Payges

Metallurgy

There's no question that the hardest part about being in a band is deciding what genre you're in. And it's even more difficult when you have to tell the other band members, at least one of whom listens mostly to smooth jazz.

Heavy Metal

The New Wave
of Heavy Metal

Nu-Metal

Rap Metal

Black Metal

Death Metal

Speed Metal

Thrash Metal

Hardcore Metal

Metalcore

Emocore

Grindcore

Noisecore

Crustcore

Industrial

Neo-Thrash

Progressive Metal

Gothic Metal

Symphonic Metal

Electro Metal

Power Metal

Dark Metal

Death Pop

Brutal Death Metal

Ambient Metal

Dark Ambient Metal

Black Ambient

Folk Metal

Doom Metal

Jazz Metal

Pagan Metal

Alternative Metal

ROCKABILLY NAMES

It just naturally helps to be born named Elvis Presley.
Because you can go ahead and make up your own rockabilly name,
just like you necessarily must make up your own punk rock name, but
you'll pretty much definitely sound like a total twit. Now, it's true that
Conway Twitty started out as Harold Jenkins, and that Sleepy LaBeef's
mother never signed off on any Arkansas birth certificate that said
"Sleepy" on it, but basically, any fool with one hand waving loose can
tell the difference. Buddy Holly is the name of a guy from Lubbock; Slim
Jim Phantom is the name of a guy from punk rock. You can get all the
flaming skulls tattooed on your forearm that you want, dudes, but only
God and your own personal mama and daddy can ever name you
Ersel Hickey.

ELVIS PRESLEY

ERSEL HICKEY

CONWAY TWITTY

BUDDY HOLLY

**BILLY LEE RILEY
AND THE LITTLE
GREEN MEN**

**GENE VINCENT
AND THE
BLUECAPS**

**CONWAY TWITTY
AND THE REDCAPS
(LATER THE
TWITTY BIRDS)**

JERRY LEE LEWIS

**MALCOLM
YELVINGTON**

**SISTER ROSETTA
THARPE**

JOHNNY CASH

CARL PERKINS

LUTHER PERKINS

**WAYNE COCHRAN
AND THE CC RIDERS**

SLEEPY LABEEF

RICKY NELSON

LONNIE MACK

ZEB TURNER

★ JERICHO JONES ★

LOUISIANA LANIS   **RED BELCHER**

BILLY *"THE KID"* EMERSON

JIMMY LEE

TEX NEIGHBORS

MAYLON HUMPHRIES

✦ **HENRY HENRY** ✦

TOMMY JIM BEAM

THE PRISONAIRES   **THE ECHOMORES**

LINDA GAIL LEWIS

WANDA JACKSON

JERRY REED

P.J. PROBY | **DUANE EDDY** | **CHARLIE FEATHERS**

RONNIE HAWKINS

JODY REYNOLDS

SID KING AND
HIS FIVE STRINGS

SONNY DECKELMAN

BILLY "CRASH"
CRADDOCK

FREDDY "BOOM-
BOOM" CANNON

NERVOUS NORVUS

SHAKIN' STEVENS

SLIM JIM PHANTOM

TAV FALCO

NARVEL FELTS

SONNY BURGESS

WARREN SMITH

JIMMY DEE

ROY HEAD

BILL HALEY

JUMPIN' GENE
SIMMONS

BOB LUMAN

BUDDY KNOX

EDDIE COCHRAN

DALE HAWKINS

AND YOU DON'T STOP

OK, all right—so sometimes you do stop. But not until long beyond the break of dawn, and definitely not until you've gone on and on. Which can be a virtue sometimes, and sometimes . . . well, it's not. The very nature of 12-inch vinyl urges you on and on in the direction of dawn—and sometimes, well . . . Hey, DJ, Could You Not Play That Song All Night Long? With a hip-hip-hippity hop?

And really, truly, it's not as if you want to stop. But unless you're the formerly Fresh Prince or Queen Latifah or LL or one of the Ices (but not the Vanilla one), the chances are that your career in what is now the hip-hop industry is going to be brief. Your career's shelf life, should you make it out of the trunk of the Benz onto any actual shelves, is likely to be quicker than the sex life of certain insects. Or, if you get really lucky, their entire life.

Which is why your hip-hop name is so very important . . . because while rap is pretty much exactly the way the latest and the greatest American argot arrives, the way slang and street talk sneak up on the radio, it's a sad truth that the latest and greatest is soon the outdatedest. There's nothing more tired and played out than being Def and Phat and full of Flava. It's like being a swingin' hepcat after The Birth Of The Cool, it's like still being groovy after all the psychedelic drugs have worn off, it's like beat-boxin' and breakin' before the next latest revival of beat-boxin' n breakin.' Although I can state for a fact that right at this very moment, beat-boxin' and breakin' are blowing up large in France . . . you might want to consider whether that's good omen or a bad one.

CAB CALLOWAY

SLIM GAILLARD

JOHN LEE HOOKER

CHUCK BERRY

MUHAMMAD ALI (FORMERLY CASSIUS CLAY)

THE LAST POETS

THE WATTS PROPHETS

GIL SCOTT-HERON

THE FATBACK BAND

DJ KOOL HERC (LATER KOOL HERC AND
THE HERCULOIDS)

DJ HOLLYWOOD

AFRIKA BAMBAATAA

GRANDMASTER FLASH (LATER GRANDMASTER
FLASH AND THE THREE MCS [INCLUDING COWBOY,
KID CREOLE, AND MELLE MEL]; THEN GRANDMASTER
FLASH AND THE FURIOUS FIVE [WITH RAHEIM,
FORMERLY MR. NESS, AND SCORPIO])

GRAND WIZARD THEODORE
& THE FANTASTIC FIVE

MEAN GENE

KOOL DJ KURT (LATER KURTIS BLOW)

GRANDMASTER CAZ AKA CASANOVA FLY

THE COLD CRUSH BROTHERS (INCLUDING ALMIGHTY KG, DJ CHARLIE CHASE, GRANDMASTER FLASH)

THE ROCK STEADY CREW

THE CRASH CREW

LADY B

THE FUNKY FOUR PLUS ONE MORE

FAB 5 FREDDY

COKE LA ROCK

TIMMY TIM

LOCKATRON JON AND SHABBA-DOO

BREAKMACHINE

UPROCK AND THE MOTOR CITY CREW

THE DYNAMIC ROCKERS

THE ROCK STEADY CREW

THE FLOORMASTERS

THE INCREDIBLE BREAKERS

THE MAGNIFICENT FORCE

THE SUGARHILL GANG (INCLUDING WONDER MIKE, BIG BANK HANK, MASTER GEE)

DJ KING TIM III

MR. MAGIC

WHODINI

LI'L RODNEY CEE

BUSY BEE STARSKI

LOVEBUG STARSKI

DISCO KING MARIO

BREAKOUT

CASANOVA FLY

EDDIE CHEEBA

DISCO WIZ

US GIRLS (INCLUDING SHA-ROCK, LISA LEE, DEBBIE DEE)

THE WORLD'S FAMOUS SUPREME TEAM (INCLUDING C-DIVINE THE MASTERMIND AND JUSTALLAH SUPERSTAR)

DISCO DADDY AND CAPTAIN RAPP

SOUL SONIC FORCE (INCLUDING AFRIKA BAMBAATAA, JAZZY JAY, MR. BIGGS, GLOBE, WHIZ KID AND POW WOW, FAB 5 FREDDY, RAMMELLZEE, AND GRANDMIXER DST & THE INFINITY RAPPERS)

GRANDMIXER D.ST.

SPOONIE GEE

DOUBLE TROUBLE

FANTASTIC FREAKS (CHIEF ROCKER
BEE, RAMMELLZEE, SHOCKDELL)

ICE-T

SCHOOLLY D

DIMPLES D

SPYDER D

RUN-DMC

BLUE CITY STRUTTERS,
AKA BOO YA TRIBE

T LA ROCK & JAZZY JAY

UTFO (UNTOUCHABLE FORCE
ORGANIZATION; INCLUDING THE
KANGOL KID, THE EDUCATED
RAPPER AKA EMD, DOCTOR ICE,
MIX MASTER ICE)

ROXANNE SHANTE'
(LATER SHANTE')

THE REAL ROXANNE
(LATER ROXANNE, LATER JOANNE
WITH THE PLAN)

SPARKY D

D.W. AND THE PARTY CREW
FEATURING ROXY

GIGOLO TONY & LACEY LACE

LITTLE ICE

THE JUICE CREW
(INCLUDING DJ MISTER CEE,
SCOOB & SCARAB LOVER)

LISA LISA & CULT JAM

KRUSH GROOVE

CRUSH GROOVE

MANTRONIX

TOO SHORT

BIZ MARKIE

THE FAT BOYS

NEWCLEUS

DOUG E. FRESH AND THE
GET FRESH CREW

THE TREACHEROUS THREE
(INCLUDING KOOL MOE DEE,
SPECIAL K, L.A. SUNSHINE,
DJ EASY LEE)

LL COOL J

SALT -N- PEPA

ERIC B & RAKIM

BOOGIE DOWN PRODUCTIONS
(INCLUDING KRS-ONE, SCOTT
LAROCK, D NICE)

DJ READY RED

SIR RAP-A-LOT

THE GETO BOYS (INCLUDING
BUSHWICK BILL, WILLIE D,
AKSHUN [AKA SCARFACE], KOOL
KEITH, CED GEE, DJ MOE)

ULTRAMAGNETIC MCS

PUBLIC ENEMY (INCLUDING
CHUCK D, FLAVOR FLAV, PROFESSOR
GRIFF, DJ TERMINATOR X)

MARLY MARL

SLICK RICK

BIG DADDY KANE

LAST ASIATIC DISCIPLES

A TRIBE CALLED QUEST
(INCLUDING Q-TIP, DJ ALI SHAHEED
MUHAMMED, JAROBI, PHIFE DAWG)

THE NATIVE TONGUES POSSE
(INCLUDING ATCQ, QUEEN LATIFAH,
THE JUNGLE BROTHERS, LEADERS OF
THE NEW SCHOOL, BLACK SHEEP)

POOR RIGHTEOUS TEACHERS

DE LA SOUL

KID 'N PLAY

HEAVY D

THE D.O.C.

2 LIVE CREW

MC HAMMER

DIGITAL UNDERGROUND

OAKTOWN 357

BUSTA RHYMES

N.W.A. (NIGGAZ WIT ATTITUDE)

CYPRESS HILL (INCLUDING
B-REAL, DJ MUGGS, SEN DOG)

MELLOW MAN ACE

HOUSE OF PAIN

FUNKDOOBIEST

THE DISPOSABLE HEROES
OF HIPHOPRISY

BRAND NUBIAN

X-CLAN

GANG STARR

ROCK STEADY DJS (INCLUDING DJ QBERT, DJ APOLLO, MIX MASTER MIKE)

DJ JAZZY JEFF AND THE FRESH PRINCE (WITH READY ROCK C)

WU-TANG CLAN (INCLUDING PRINCE [THE RZA] RAKEEM, RAEKWON, OL' DIRTY BASTARD, METHOD MAN, GHOST FACE KILLAH, GENIUS [GZA], U-GOD, MASTER KILLA, INSPECTAH DECK)

FUNKMASTER FLEX

DR. DRE

DR. DEF

DR. FRESHH

DR. COLD GETTIN DUMB

MOBB DEEP (PRODIGY AND HAVOC)

COMMON

WARREN G

BONE THUGS -N- HARMONY

MISSY "MISDEMEANOR" ELLIOTT

SLICK RICK

KRISS KROSS

ANOTHER BAD CREATION (ABC)

MC LYTE

ANTOINETTE

THE BEASTIE BOYS

THE PHARCYDE

THE FUGEES (AKA THE REFUGEE ALL STARS)

ORGANIZED KONFUSION

THE NOTORIOUS B.I.G (BIGGIE SMALLS)

SNOOP DOGGIE DOGG

FAT JOE

BIG L

ONYX

BOOT CAMP CLIK

TUPAC SHAKUR (PREVIOUSLY 2PAC)

NAS

JAY-Z

DMX

jeru the
damaja

METHOD MAN

REDMAN

MASE

PUFF DADDY
LATER PUFFY, THEN P. DIDDY

48

TALIB KWELI

MOS DEF

PHAROAHE MONCH

NAUGHTY BY NATURE

OUTSIDAZ

SLUM VILLAGE

SCARFACE

LI'L JON & THE EASTSIDE BOYZ

THE YING YANG TWINS

50 CENT

JA RULE

TRICK DADDY

LUDACRIS

OUTKAST

AKON

THE OUTLAWZ

CHAMILLIONAIRE

MR. LIF

AKROBATIK

TERMANOLOGY

M-DOT

VIRTUOSO

KABIR

SUPRALIMINAL

BENZINO

TRIPLE THREAT

MADE MEN

ED O.G

THE CLIPSE

FAM-LAY

TIMBALAND

MASTER P

JUVENILE

LIL WAYNE

C-MURDER

MYSTIKAL

MIA X

BABY BOY DA PRINCE

5TH WARD WEEBIE

CHEEKY BLAKK

DJ JUBILEE

GHETTO TWINZ

HOT BOYS

MANNIE FRESH

MS. TEE

MURDER INC	DJ MUGGS
SOULJA SLIM	DJ CLUE
SILKK THE SHOCKER	DJ FOCUS
REV RUN	DJ QBERT
REV. RAP	DJ INFAMOUS
PASTOR TROY	DJ POLO
PID (PREACHAS IN DISGUISE)	LIL' KIM
SFC (SOLDIERS FOR CHRIST)	FOXY BROWN
DOC (DISCIPLES OF CHRIST)	THE ROOTS
GOSPEL GANGSTAZ	HI-TEK
JEDI MIND TRICKS	DILATED PEOPLES
MIMS	THE COUP
FABOLOUS	OOBIE
UNCLE MURDER	LIL SCRAPPY
DJ PREMIER	LIL WYTE
DJ SCRATCH	YOUNG JEEZY
DJ QUIK	PETEY PABLO
DJ PETE ROCK	PROJECT PAT

SOULJA BOY
THREE 6 MAFIA
YOUNGBLOODZ
AL KAPONE
ARRESTED DEVELOPMENT
CUNNINLYNGUISTS
GOODIE MOB
LIL BOOSIE
LIL FLIP · PIMP C
SCREWED UP CLICK
MC SHY D
WITCHDOCTOR
YO MAJESTY
Z-RO
FAMOUS

Tune Town or

Smell the Three-Fingered Glove: The Mythical Band Names of the Mythical Bands of Film, TV, Cartoons, and uh, Myth

Naming your band is the easy part. There are other elements of the glorious struggle that are less glorious than strugglish. A whole lot of being in a band is like disassembling your drum set and putting it all in the trunk of your car except for the kick drum that has to go in the passenger seat because it doesn't fit in the trunk, and then taking it all out and schlepping it over to Gary's dad's den to practice and having to put it all together again, and then finding out that you're not gonna practice because Trevor the bass player is still mad from the last time and didn't want to talk to anybody in the band ever again so he on purpose didn't call to say he's totally quitting for good this time, for sure.

So probably you'd think it would be way easier being in a cartoon band on TV, but if anything, it's even worse. True, there are probably fewer sound checks, but there's just generally a lot more drama. Teenage cavegirls tear your tiger-skin suits right off you . . . your band's matching dune buggies all go flying right off the end of the pier, one after another . . . talent scouts from Hollywood sign you and then tear up your contract and jump all over the shreds . . . the other chimps chew up your tambourine . . . your records don't really get released but only come out on the back of cereal boxes . . . ghosts (groovy ones, perhaps, but super-scary just the same) freak out all your band members on the night of The Big Talent Show . . . and beyond any of that, worst of all, your drummers keep spontaneously exploding.

The Monkees

The New Monkees

Lancelot Link and The Evolution Revolution

Gorillaz

The Partridge Family

The Cowsills

The Von Trapp Family Singers

The Carrie Nations (formerly The Kelly Affair)

The Archies

The Banana Splits

The Bugaloos

The Groovie Ghoulies

Kaptain Kool and the Kongs

The Hardy Boys Plus 3

Frankenstein Jr. and The Impossibles

The Neptunes (with Jabberjaw)

The Bedrock Rollers (with Pebbles and Bamm-Bamm)

The Way-Outs

The Beau Brummelstones

The Beasties

The BC-52s

The Bedbugs

Collect 'em all!!

AS SEEN ON TV

Alvin and the Chipmunks

Melvin and the Squirrels

The Chipettes

Sgt. Pepper's Lonely Hearts Club Band
(featuring the one and only Billy Shears)

The Chan Clan

Butch Cassidy and the Sundance Kids

The Brady Kids (aka The Kids from The Brady Bunch;
formerly the Silver Platters, the Brady 6,
later The Banana Convention)

The Beagles

The California Raisins

Fat Albert and the Cosby Kids

The Catanooga Cats

MC Skat Kat

Jem and the Holograms (versus The Misfits)

Barbie and the Rockers

The Be Sharps

Party Posse

The New Kids In A Ditch

The Rappin' Rabbis

Testament

Kovenant (formerly Satanica)

Captain Bart and the Tequila Mockingbirds

MC Safety and the Caution Crew

Hooray For Everything

Crazy Backwards Alphabet

The Larry Davis Experience
(formerly The Larry Davis Dance Kings)

Spiñal Tap (formerly the Creatures, the Lovely Lads, the Originals [litigation], then the New Originals, then the Thamesmen, then the Dutchmen, the Rave Breakers, the Flamin' Daemons, the Shiners, the Mondos, the Doppel Gang, the People, Loose Lips, Waffles, Hot Waffles, Silver Service, Biscuits, Love Biscuits, the Mud Below, The Tufnel-St. Hubbins Group, later Anthem [litigation], The Cadburys, then Spiñal Tap again, then Spiñal Tap Mark II [litigation], currently Spiñal Tap)

The Wally Hung Trio
(later the Wally Hung Experience)

Duke Fame and the Fame Throwers

Camel Lips

O-Town

The Twobadours

The Folksmen

The Main Street Singers

The Ramblers

Hub Kapp and the Wheels

The Ladmo Trio

The Munchkins

Commodore Condello's Salt River Navy Band

The One and Only Genuine Original Family Band

Cane and the Stubborn Stains

Cherry Bomb

Ming Tea

Martha Reader and the Vowelles

The Blowholes

The Blow-Waves

Otis Day and the Knights

The Blues Brothers

The Good Ole Boys

Murph and the Magictones

The Louisiana Gator Boys

The Shitty Beatles

The Exploding Pintos

Dujour

The Grinning Americans

The Little White Girls Blues Quartet

Marvin Berry and the Starlighters

The Horndogs

Satan's Penis

While supplies last!

The Shmenge Brothers

The Happy Wanderers

The Redcoats

Wyld Stallions

The Lone Rangers

Leather and the Suedes

Lester Crabtree and the Three Crabs

The Jolly Green Giants

The Four Martians

The Sugar Bears

The Four Swine

The Dale Gribble Bluegrass Experience

The Alabama Porch Monkeys

The Mau Maus

The Rutles

Toad the Wet Sprocket

The Soggy Bottom Boys

Lenny and the Squigtones

The Stains

Stillwater

Sven Helstrom and the Swedish Rhythm Kings

Alice Bowie

The Committments
(formerly And And! And, later The Brazzers)

Zack Attack

Buckaroo Bonzai and the Hong Kong Cavaliers

Max Frost and the Troopers

Chris Gaines

Autobahn

The Wombles

The Gnats

The Mosquitos

The Honeybees

The International Silver String Submarine Band

The Dirty Mops

Ruben and The Jets

The Kenosha Kickers

The Banned (formerly Dog Market)

California Dreams

The Wonders (formerly The Oneders, later The Heardsmen)

The Cheetah Girls

Dingos Ate My Baby

Dr. Teeth and The Electric Mayhem

FREE!
INSIDE SPECIALLY MARKED BOXES

The Five Heartbeats

Kidd Videos

Mystik Spiral

Platinum Weird

Chicky Baby, No Cool Cat, and Dirty Dog

The Queen Haters

The Rock-afire Explosion

Bear Country Jamboree

Crucial Taunt

Steel Dragon

Scrantonicity

School of Rock

Tenacious D

Fingerbang

MVPS:

Johnny Napalm

Judy Nails

Axel Steel

Izzy Sparks

Casey Lynch

Lars Ümlaut

Xavier Stone

Punk

or, We Came, We Played, We Slept on Your Floor

So the great thing about punk is this: There's No Rules, dude! We mean it, man!

Well, maybe some. A few. Just a couple. Like one or two, maybe. Like if you call it punk rock, well, then it's officially gotta rock. It can't have like keyboards or saxophones or something. Because then it would be . . . well, lame. Or new wave, and thus lame too. Or post-punk, and then it's boring. Really, really boring.

And if it's hardcore punk, there's a bunch more rules. About haircuts and how fast you gotta play, and various things, and details about not having catchy choruses and verses both—you can have one, maybe, but not the other, and really it's better if it all just sounds the same—all these rules being based on what was gnarly and rad and other Southern California terms, as heard from the outskirt suburbs of Washington, DC, from about 1980 or so. And if it's straight-edge, then there's even more rules and you can't break any of them ever, forever, for the rest of your life. Forever. Or at least until the next time you get drunk.

And if it's positive punk, there's rules but they're all pretty bendy and flexy. And positive! Sort of the same for peace punk, but it's more political than positive—it's kind of hard to be both, at least simultaneously. And if it's emo, well, then it's not really punk, then, is it? It's all trendy and too many girls come to the shows and . . . well, OK, that's kind of why we're thinking of switching over to being kind of somewhat Emocore. But with a really edgy kind of hardcore, straight-edge attitude. But only with more cute girls coming to the shows. So we're maybe going to have to change our haircuts. But other than that, we're always gonna be Punk 4 Ever! No Rules! Anarchy!

Except for when it comes to names. 'Cause there, in that case, there's rules, eternal rules. Lots of 'em. And they're like totally meaningful. So screw you! Go buy us some beer.

Hound Dog Taylor and the House Rockers

The MC5

The Stooges (then Iggy And The Stooges, then Iggy Pop)

The New York Dolls

The Modern Lovers

Suicide

The Ramones (previously The Tangerine Puppets, Sniper, Butch, later MCDD)

The Dictators

The Heartbreakers

Television

Richard Hell and the Voidoids

The Patti Smith Group

Blondie

Talking Heads

The Saints

Radio Birdman

The Negatives

Rocket From the Tombs

The Dead Boys

Pere Ubu

The Electric Eels

DEVO

The Cramps

The Real Kids

Tuff Darts

The Shirts

The Mumps

The Miamis

Wayne County and
the Electric Chairs
(later Jayne County and the Electric Chairs)

The Laughing Dogs

Mink DeVille

The Testors

The Senders

Teenage Jesus and the Jerks

The Contortions

James Black and the Whites

The Swankers

The Sex Pistols (previously The Strand, The Swankers; names considered included Le Bomb, Subterraneans, Teenage Novel, and Beyond, later The Spots, [Sex Pistols On Tour Secretly], The Rich Kids, Public Image, Ltd [PIL], The Greedy Bastards, The Vicious White Kids, The Ex Pistols, The Professionals, Chequered Past, The Chiefs of Relief, The Neurotic Outsiders, The Philistines, Man-Raze)

The Damned

The Clash

The Buzzcocks

The Stranglers

X Ray Spex

The Subway Sect

Wire

The Unwanted

The Adicts

The Cockney Rejects

The Radiators
From Space

Slaughter & the Dogs

Chelsea

Eater

Johnny Moped

Ed Banger & the
Nosebleeds

Johnny and the
Self Abusers

The Pork Dukes

Penetration

The Adverts

Generation X

THE JAM

The Members

999

THE 222'S

SHAM 69

ANGELIC UPSTARTS

Stiff Little Fingers

EDDIE AND THE HOT RODS

The Boomtown Rats

The Vibrators

The Rezillos

SIOUXSIE AND THE BANSHEES

The Flowers of Romance

THE SLITS

The Au Pairs

The Boys

The Cortinas

The Lurkers

Abrasive Wheels

The Mekons

GANG OF FOUR

Peter and the Test Tube Babies

METAL URBAIN

Stinky Toys

The Weirdos

The Screamers

The Consumers

The Liars

The Germs

The Bags

The Dils

X

The Plugz

The Alley Cats

Black Randy and
the Metrosquad

The Dickies

The Zeros

Los Olividados

Los Illegals

The Brat

Thee Undertakers

The Eyes

The Gears

The Deadbeats

The Flesh Eaters

The Gun Club

The Urinals

The Randoms

The Nuns

The Avengers

The Mutants

Crime

DOA

The Subhumans

Dogs of War

The Adolescents

The Chiefs

Angry Samoans
(previously Vom)

The Smog Marines

Bad Brains

The Controllers

Agent Orange

The Descendents

China White

MIA

Würm

Black Flag

The Minutemen

Saccharine Trust

The Circle Jerks

Social Distortion

Social Decay

Social Unrest

Social Suicide

Social Spit

Anti Social

F Word

P.A.L.

Rhino 39

Middle Class

The Mau Maus

The Mads

The Mad Parade

The Mad Society

Circle One

Castration Squad

Nervous Gender

The Hard Ons

Redd Kross

TSOL (True Sound of
Liberty or True Sons
of Liberty)

DI

Negative Trend

No Trend

Negative Element

Negative Approach

Negative Gain

Channel 3

Rabid

Active Dogs

The Scabs

The Scars

The Skulls

The Skrews

The Skids

The Stains

The Sins

The Ruts

The Crowd

The Crewd

Bad Religion

Fear

Fang

Flipper

The Contractions

Free Beer

The Fuck Ups

Negative Trend

7 Seconds

Los Microwaves

Frightwig

The Feederz

JFA (previously
Jodie Foster s Army)

The Meat Puppets

The Junior
Chemists

The Advocats

Bang Gang

The Big Boys

Cringe

The Dicks

The Skunks

DRI

MDC (Millions of Dead Cops police
trouble resulted , then Multi Death
Corporation, then Millions of Dead
Children, then Milllions of Dead
Christians, then Millions of Damn
Christians, then Millions of Dead
Chickens, then, for some reason,
Millions of Dead Contractors, then
Metal Devil Cokes, then Magnus
Dominus Corpus, then MDC Unplugged)

Jerry s Kidz

Snot

Verbal Abuse

Diet of Worms

The Crucifucks

The Meatmen

The Misfits

Fried Abortions

Hugh Beaumont
Experience

Fearless Iranians
From Hell

The Vandals

The Mentors

Urban Idles

Minor Threat

Fugazi

Hüsker Dü

Idle Threat

Loud Fast Rules

The Clitboys

The Crusties

Die Kreuzen

Articles of Faith

The Effigies

The Wasted

Wasted Brains

Wasted Youth

Youth Brigade

Youth Gone Mad

Impatient Youth

Bored Youth

Pleased Youth

Dead Youth

Youth of Today

Youth Quake

Youth Patrol

Reagan Youth

Young and Useless

Negative Trend

No Trend

White Flag
White Cross
White Trash
White Boy
The Necros
The Fastbacks
Dag Nasty
The Melvins
Monitor
Wall of Voodoo
Bpeople
Human Hands
Vox Pop
45 Grave
March of Crimes
Poison Idea
The Wipers

Anti Scrunti Faction
Sick Of It All
The Beastie Boys
The Abused
The Fiends
The Plasmatics
The Cro Mags
Agnostic Front
The Lunachicks
The Celibate Rifles
The Dub Pistols
The Dead Milkmen
The Dayglo Abortions
The Nils
Fat and Fucked Up
Murphy's Law
The Corpse Grinders
Crucial Truth
NOFX
Rancid
Sublime

Rockin' Royalty

Subtle and strange, strange and subtle are the pearlescent words of the poet. Mysterious and mystical too. And all that goes at least probably double when it comes to naming your band. There are like three hundred ways to go wrong—three thousand, ten thousand, ten million, zillion. A lot. And then there you are, way off track with your band's dumb-ass name on the flyer somewhere below "Free Beer."

Anyway, poetry is what is on our minds mostly when we name our bands. And since many of us slept through that part of English class, we go for pomp and majesty. And grandiosity. Stuff like that.

The Monarchs

The Teen Kings

The Teenage Kings of Harmony (*later including members of The Chosen Gospel Singers, The Pilgrim Travelers*)

The Teen Queens

The Royal Teens

The Royal Guards

The Royal Guardsmen

The Five Royales

The Royalettes

The Royal Debs

Lorraine and the Socialites

Nero and the Gladiators

Caesar and the Centurions

Sam the Sham and the Pharoahs

The Commodores

The Nozblemen

The Bishops

The Counts

The Count Bishops

The Earls

The Dukes

The Dukes of Earl

The Pleasure Barons

The Pageboys

The Jesters

Queen

King Harvest

King Crimson

The Surf Kings

The Bop Kings

The Boogie Kings

The Kingsmen

The Funky Kings

The Little Kings

The Kings of Soul

✦

The King Casuals

✦

King Biscuit Boy

✦

Kings of Leon

✦

The Kings of Convenience

✦

King Curtis and the King Pins

✦

Kingsize Taylor and the Dominos

✦

The Rocking Kings

✦

The Rhythm Kings

✦

The New Orleans Rhythm Kings

✦

Jelly Roll Morton and the New Orleans Rhythm Kings

✦

The Chicago Rhythm Kings

✦

Ike Turner and His Kings of Rhythm

✦

Bill Wyman and the Rhythm Kings

✦

The Cobalt Rhythm Kings

✦

Martin and His Rhythm Kings

✦

The New Kings of Rhythm

FOLK IN A

Some of the finest, firmest, least-fattening of all American music, the stirring songs that America sang when its workers, its farmers, its fishermen, and its firemen all went arm in arm to nightclubs and coffeehouses, that music was what we called folk. We called it folk because we don't listen to it that much, and because it's a nice and short and simple and convenient name for something we don't know what else to call it. Folk, as you know, was probably best played in groups. It was safer that way, and made it less certain that you would get beat up by jazzbos and rockers and fierce classical cellists. And when you formed a group, the chances were pretty strong that you called it something that ended in either the words "Singers" or "Trio." Because if folk is about anything, it's about tradition and the lack of originality.

The Almanac Singers

The Weavers

The Kingston Trio

The New Christy Minstrels

Peter, Paul, and Mary

The Rooftop Singers

The Gateway Singers

The Gaslight Singers

The Serendipity Singers

The Whiskey Hill Singers

The Hillside Singers

The Silver Gate Singers

The Four Freshman

The BroThers Four

The SmoThers BroThers

The CounTry GenTlemen

The Tarriers

The Lincolns

New LosT CiTy Ramblers

The ShanTyboys

The SeaEarers

The YachTsmen

The Gondoliers

The Windjammers

The Seekers

The New Seekers

The Sandpipers

The Bachelors

The Barons

The Banjo Jokers

The Banjo Barons

The Coachmen

The BabysiTTers

The Undergrads

The WayFarers

The Wanderin' Five

The Homesteaders

The Pine Toppers

The Jim Kweskin Jug Band

The Even Dozen Jug Band

The Jug Band Project

The Minstrels Three

The Big Three

The HaliFax 3

The Cumberland 3

The Appalachians

The Westside 4

The Just IV

The Mugwumps

The Mamas & The Papas

The Heightsmen

The Highwaymen

The Journeymen

Ian & Sylvia (later, The Great Speckled Bird)

The Kentucky Colonels

The Easy Riders

The Irish Rovers

The Dubliners

The Charles River Boys

Randy Sparks and The Back Porch MajoriTy

Kenny Rodgers and The FirsT EdiTion

Up WiTh People

Simon & GarEunkel

The WolEe Tones

FairporT ConvenTion

STeeleye Span

PlanxTy

Horslips

The STrawbs

The Yeomen

The Moonshiners

The Milburnaires

The Swagmen

The Swingin' 6

The Sunshine Company

The Talismen

Three Young Men From MonTana

The Village STompers

LITTLE BUT LOUD

There's little to be said here. There's a career to be made, if your dad has managerial inclinations, as the youngest and smallest and blondest of all the blues harp players in Phoenix, Arizona. Best start that career now, li'l junior, and get yourself a personal certified public accountant that your dad can't stand. And do it all soon, because before you know it, your voice is going to change, your beard is going to sprout, your dad and you are in court for decades, and you're dyeing your gray-flecked hair as blond as it's ever going to get again. And you're just another of the herds of blues harp dudes of Phoenix, and now there's some damn eight-year-old harmonica whiz on the scene that everybody's talking about . . .

Little Richard

Little Walter

Little Eva

Little Esther

Little Eller

Little Evelyn

Little Willie John

Little Sonny

Little Ced

Little Clifford

Little Stevie Wonder

Little Anthony & The Imperials

Little Steven and the Disciples of Soul

Little Caesar and the Consuls

Tommie Little and the Sunrise Rangers

Little Virginia and Her Virginians

Little Buster

Little Anne

Little Barbara

Little Joe

Little Joe y La Familia (later Little Joe y La Mafia)

Little Brenda Lee

Little Peggy March

Little Jimmy Osmond

Little Gary Ferguson

Little John

Little John and the Merrymen

Li'l Jon

Li'l Rob

Li'l Romeo

Li'l D

Li'l Wayne

Li'l Bow Wow

Li'l Kim

Li'l Mama

Lil iROCC

Li'l Troy

Li'l Andy

Li'l Cease

Li'l Rascal

Li'l Tykes

Li'l Precious

Little Feat

Little River Band

Little Texas

The Little Ones

The Little Kings

Tony Little

Big Tiny Little

Tiny Tim

Wee Willie Williams

REGGAE NAMES

It's possible that the reggae name is the absolute Abyssinian apotheosis of the self-declared showbiz name. But maybe not. Because album titles alone, not merely the gorgeous language and grooves they represent but the mere album titles alone . . . whoa, if poetry be the spark of the soul, spark that chalice up, man. Whoa!

For who, who among us, can win when a man as great as U-Roy, with a name as great as U-Roy, puts out a record as nuancedly titled as *Ace From Out of Space*? When Dennis Alcapone points out *My Voice Is Insured For Half A Million Dollars*? When Burning Spear—who among us doesn't wished we'd named ourselves "Burning Spear" before Winston Rodney snagged it?—releases *Living Dub Vol. 1*, and then confounds and trumps and confuses everyone across the earth with *Living Dub Vol. II*? Dr. Alimentado, easily one of the finest practitioners of his own particular aural specialty, will likely for all time and eternity see himself eclipsed by a title so pure, so powerful, so perfect, so poetic that who among us, having heard it, can say they wouldn't care to be "The Best Dressed Chicken In Town?"

Count Ossie

Count Busty

Duke Reid

Sir Coxsone Dodd

Sir Lord Comic and His Cowboys

Lord Creator

Lord Brynner

Lord Tanamo

Lord Sassafras

Ruddy, Supreme Ruler
of Sound

Prince Buster

Prince Lincoln

Prince Alla

Prince Far I
(previously Prince Cry Cry)

Prince Jammy

Prince Jazzbo

King Tubby

King Chubby

King Sporty

King Cannon

King Shark

King Stitt

King Apparatus

Kid Gungo

Junior Soul

Junior Delgado

Junior Murvin

Junior Marvin

Doctor Ring Ring

Dr. Alimantado

Mr. Versatile

Mr. Foundation

Funny Man

Dandy

Dandy Livingstone

Gallimore Sutherland

Beresford Ricketts

Lascelles Perkins

Theophilius Beckford

Hopeton Thaxter

Shenley Duffus

Millie Small
Max Romeo
Dennis Alcapone
Lone Ranger
Mystic Bowie
Roland Alphonso
Rico Rodriguez
Ansel Collins
Toots Hibbert
Niney The Observer
Clint Eastwood
Django
General Saint
Clue J
Cuddly T
Bunny & Ruddy
Bunny & Skitter
Chuck & Darby
Chuck & Dobby
Freddie & Fitzy
Lloyd & Randolph

Scientist
The Mad Professor
Ras Allah
Ras Michael
Pluto Shervington
Tapper Zukie
Lloyd Charmers
Errol Scorcher
Desmond Dekker
Stranger Cole
Stranger and Ken
Stranger & Patsy
Strangejah
Joe Gibbs
Joe Higgs
Lee "Scratch" Perry
Girl Satchmo
Bunny Wailer
Bunny Lee
Bunny Maloney

IVAN YAP
BURNING SPEAR
RANKING DREAD
RANKING TREVOR
RANKING JOE
JAH JOE
RAS MIDAS
GENERAL ECHO
BOBBY MELODY
DELROY MELODY
JAH STITCH
MICHAEL PROPHET
CAPTAIN SINBAD
U-ROY
I-ROY
TRINITY

Big Youth	Barrington Levy
Tony Tuff	Sugar Minott
Papa Levi	Buju Banton
Papa Tarzan	Shabba Ranks
Michigan & Smiley	Shaggy
Nigger Kojak	Macka B
Dillinger	Mikey Dread
Sly Dunbar	Donna & Althea
Robbie Shakespeare	Augustus Pablo
Leroy "Horseface" Wallace	Bob Andy
Flabba Holt	Horace Andy
Bingy Bunny	The Mexicano
Mikey Chung	
Style Scott	

AN INCREDIBLE TRIBUTE TO:

You probably think being in a tribute band is easy, don't you? But that's far from the truth—if anything, it's harder to be in a tribute band than a regular band. A lot harder. Way harder. Much harder. Even more hard.

It's true that you don't have to waste a lot of time writing all new tuneage, that you can just practice along with the albums—but hold it right there—because which albums should you practice along with? Say, for instance you absolutely finally decide you're going to be An Incredible Tribute to Bon Scott–Era AC/DC and also to Van Halen, pre–Sammy Hagar. Sure, choosing a name seems easy enough with a masterstroke like AC/DC/VH1 (which was one of those inspired-by-God-after-the-second-six-pack moments (you should totally see our logo, dude!)) but think about the challenges that come after the name-choice ceremonies and all.

Because it's only when you begin to explore all the Incredible Tribute possibilities that you start to realize how truly different Bon Scott–era AC/DC and pre–Sammy Hagface Van Halen truly are. And that's not even getting into how differently the lead guitar guy has to dress on a song-by-song basis if you try to mix the set up a little bit. (Eventually, you learn that it's best to do one entire set of him as Eddie Van Halen, and another entirely separate set of him skipping around as Angus in his little schoolboy shorts.) Because while it's possible to do both, especially if the lead singer is doing David Lee Roth, because that can absorb vital offstage costume-change time, it can be a little difficult for the audience to get their heads around, especially since a lot of them have been drinking out by their cars and stuff. And by the time they come back inside, and maybe they smoked a doobie too, well . . . it's like there's a whole different band playing, or at least a whole different lead guitar player scooting around in shorts and when they stepped outside he was Eddie Van Halen and all. Which some people feel can be confusing. (Although many of our fans find that this ADDS A LOT to the show . . .)

93

ABBAlicious

ABBAcadabra

ABBAgirls (all-girl ABBA tribute duo)

ABBAbabes (all-girl ABBA tribute duo)

ABBA Dabba Doo

ABBAgold (aka the Real ABBA Gold)

ABBAmania (Scotland's only true ABBA tribute)

ABBA-like

ABBA-mania

ABBA Mania

ABBAlanche

ABBA UK

ABBArrival

Arrival

ABBA World Revival (Czech Republic)

ABBA Revolution

BABBA

FABBA

GABBA (tribute to ABBA in the style of the Ramones)

ABBAsolutely (All-Stars)

ABBAsolutely Live

Rebjorn

Bjorn Again

A*Teens (formerly ABBATeens)

ABBA XMas

Dancing ABBA (in German)

Rosvikskoren

San Francisco Gay Men's Chorus (tribute album ExtrABBAganza)

ABBAMAGIC ("The best tribute to ABBA I have ever seen or heard," Ronnie Wood of the Rolling Stones)

Waterloo (Sweden)

Mamma Mia - It's Almost ABBA

ABBA Inferno

Swede Dreams

AC/Dshe (the only all-girl tribute to Bon Scott-era AC/DC)

Hell's Belle's (all-female AC/DC tribute band)

OC/DC (Orange County, CA)

BC/DC (British Columbia)

RayC/BC (North Vancouver, BC)

LA/DC (Los Angeles, CA)

FA/KE (Germany)

AC/Seedy

Hayseed Dixie (AC/DC done bluegrass style)

AC/Do

Acdsie

AB/CDS YOU WILL F

Bonfire (Los Angeles, CA; advertised as, "An incredible tribute to AC/DC during the Bon Scott-era.")

Bonfire (Cleveland, OH; Bon Scott-era)

Bonfire (Chicago, IL; Bon Scott-era)

Bonfire (Ireland)

Bon Ded (Modesto, CA)

Highway to Hell (Sydney, Australia)

Highway To Hell (Tampa, FL)

High Voltage (SF)

Hail Caesar

ACCA DACCA ("We Are The World's Greatest Ever AC/DC Bon Scott Tribute, Bar None. These Are Mighty Strong Words However We Can Back Them Up.")

BACCA

Bare Rump (tribute to AC/DC featuring a female Angus and a female singer)

American Thighs (all-girl AC/DC tribute)

ThundHerStruck (all-female AC/DC tribute with guest visits from former AC/DC drummer Chris Slade)

Whole Lotta Rosies (all-female AC/DC tribute band)

D OUT

Aeromyth

Eurosmith

Aeroforce

AeroRocks

Ladysmith (Hollywood's all-girl tribute to Aerosmith)

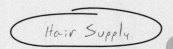

Hair Supply

The Australian Bob Marley Show

The Australian Eagles Show

The Australian Blues Brothers Show

The Australian Van Morrison Show

The Australian Black Sabbath Show

The Australian Status Quo Show

The Australian Doors Show

The Australian U2 Show

The Australian Pearl Jam Show

The Australian Stones Show

The Australian Kiss Show

The Australian Status Quo

The Australian Hothouse Flowers

Blondee
Blondie and Beyond
Bleach
Once More Into the Bleach
Heart of Glass
Atomic
The Atomics
The Parallel Lines
Gentlemen Prefer Blondie

Alike Cooper

Malice Cooper

Fistful of Alice

Just Alice

Alice Troopers

Mr. Nice Guy

No More Mr. Nice Guy

Alias Cooper the Billion Dollar Baby ("A Cincinnati-based tribute to Alice Cooper AND Ozzy Osbourne with Black Sabbath in one night.")

THE ALMOST BROTHERS BAND

The Beached Boys

The Beach Toys

The Beach Bums

The Beach Buddies

The Sunny Boys (Italy)

The Beach Boys Inc (UK)

The Brighton Beach Boys (UK)

96

THE BEATALLS

THE BEATALL

THE BEATELS

THE BAETLES

THE CHEAT BEATLES

THE CHEATLES

THE OTHER BEATLES

THE BEETLES UK

THE JAPANESE BEATLES

THE BANDIT BEATLES

THE ZEATLES (NEW ZEALAND)

THE BLUE BEATLES

THE SILVER BEATS (JAPAN)

THE FAUX FOUR

THE FAB FAUX

SGT. PEPPER'S ONLY DART BOARD BAND

THE MERSEY BEATLES (LIVERPOOL, ENGLAND)

THE BUGS (ROME, ITALY)

THE STINGLESS (MILAN, ITALY)

THE ROACHES

EPPSTEIN PLANNING PARTY (JAPAN)

THE FAB 5 (JAPAN)

MEET THE DONTACOS (JAPAN)

THE BEATLEG (JAPAN)

BEAT THE MEETLES (DENMARK)

BEATALLICA (BEATLES/METALLICA TRIBUTE)

BEATLEMANIACS

BEATLEMANIA NOW

THE CAVERNERS

LIVERPOOL LADS

THE FAB FOUR

THE UPBEAT BEATLES

THE OTHER BEATLES

THE BARGAIN BEATLES ("PLAYING THE SONGS IN THE ORIGINAL KEYS")

BEATLE TEST (BEATLES AND AC/DC TRIBUTE)

Vital Idol

Hillbilly Idol

Black McSabbath

Slack Sabbath

Sack Blabbath

Slack Babbath

Mack Sabbath

Mac Sabbath

Sabbath Bloody Sabbath

Back Stabbath

Black Bettie (all-female Black Sabbath)

Mistress of Reality

Sabotage

Sabbra Caddabra

Bat Soup (The best Brazilian Ozzy Osbourne tribute band.)

Born Again (Black Sabbath)

The Ozzybournes

Oz-Mosis

Crazy Babies

Rebourne

Speak of the Devil (tribute to Ozzy and Black Sabbath)

Blooze Brothers

The Alabama Blues Brothers
(Huntsville, AL; actual brothers)

The Birmingham Blues Brothers
(England)

Klapstuk Feestband (Blues Brothers tribute; Netherlands)

The Blues Broads

The Bruised Brothers

The Blues Busters

The Bootleg Blues Brothers

The Copenhagen Blues Brothers

The Blues Brothers UK

The Scottish Blues Brothers

The "Illinois" Blues Brothers
(UK)

Briefcase Blues

Alias Elwood and Jake

The Bruce Brothers
(tribute to the Blues Brothers and Bruce Springsteen)

Bon Giovi

By Jovi

Born Jovi

Bon Jovie

Jovi

Kon Chauvi

Bad Medicine (Glendale Heights, IL)

Bad Medicine (Deer Park, NY)

Bad Obsession (Modena, Italy)

Bad Obsession (Montreal, Quebec)

Bad Obsession (Glos, UK)

Bon Journey (Bon Jovi/Journey tribute)

New Jersey (Australia)

The Karpenters (UK)

The Larpenteurs (Minnesota)

The Carpetones

Carpenters Magic (UK)

Carpenters Interpretations (UK)

Yesterday Once More

Britney . . . One More Time (Canada; "North America's Best Tribute to Britney Spears–this performer can't be touched.")

Britney Did It Again (Canada)

Britney (Canada)

Bruce Springstein and the East Street Band

The B Street Band (Asbury Park, NJ)

Bruce in the USA (Las Vegas, NV)

THE CLASHED

THE TRASH

COUNTER CLASH

LONDON CALLING

STRUMMERVILLE

BLACK MARKET CLASH

COMBAT ROCK— THE CLASH TRIBUTE

THE CLASH CITY ROCKERS

CLASHBACK

THE MAGNIFICENT SEVEN

The Conmitments

The Kommitments

The Ten Commitments

The Other Commitments

Coolplay

Coldplace

Coldplayd

Crowded Scouse
(Liverpool, England)

Creedence Clearwater Recycled

Creedence Clearwater Revisited
(featuring former members of
Creedence Clearwater Revival and
the guitar player from The Cars;
post-lawsuit)

Green River Revival

Cajun Country Revival (Australia)

Camp David

Space Oddity

Ziggy Barlust

Deepest Purple (UK)

Deeper Than Purple (Austria)

Cheap Purple (Germany)

Cheap Purple (UK)

Cheap Turtle (Germany)

Child In Time (Germany)

Child In Time (Sweden)

Come Taste The Band (Norway)

Purple Rainbow (Holland)

Peep Durple (Germany)

Perfect Strangers (Norway)

Perfect St. Rangers (Spain)

Perfect Street Rangers (Norway)

Shades of Purple (UK)

Shades of Purple (Germany)

Shades of Deep Purple (Germany)

Taste of Purple (UK)

Made In Japan (US)

Burn (Germany)

Hush (Italy)

Def Repplica

Deft Leppard

High N Dry ("Hottest Def Leppard Tribute in Texas! Maybe the only.")

Jef Leppard

Hysteria

Hysteria (Rhode Island)

Hysteria CT (Connecticut)

Skinny Leonard

DEXY'S MIDNIGHT OASIS

Diana Boss and the Extremes (Australia)

dixie chicklets

chicks with dixie

The Doorz

Morrison Hotel

The Soft Parade

Peace Frog

Wild Child

L.A. Doors (Los Angeles, CA)

LA Doors (UK)

The Bootleg Doors

The BackDoors

The Doors of Perception

The Celebration of the Lizard

The Clone Doors

The Crystal Doors

Riders on the Storm (featuring Robbie Krieger and Ray Manzarek of the Doors and Ian Astbury of The Cult, then Brett Scallions of Fuel; previously known as The Doors of the 21st Century until The Doors'—then D21C—drummer sued)

Mojo Risin'

Duran Duran Duran

Doctor Duran

The Illegal Eagles

Spread Eagle

The Beagles

Hotel California

JERRY'S KIDS

SHAKEDOWN STREET

DARK STAR ORCHESTRA

CUBENSIS

BOKUMARU

THE DEADBEATS

ALLIGATOR

BORDER LEGION

CLOUD 9

COSMIC CHARLIES (UK)

MIRACLE TICKET

GREAT NORTH SPECIAL

JAKE'S LEG

MIDNITE BLUE

THE NOODLES

SPLINTERED SUNLIGHT

THE DRUIDS

THE WEBS

UNCLE JOHN'S BAND

DED GUISE

Earth Wind Desire

Earth Wind For Hire

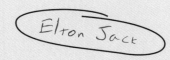

Elton Jack

Fake No More (Faith No More tribute)

Fleetwood Bac

Fleetwood Max

Rumours

Rumours–The Legend of Fleetwod Mac (Santa Clara, CA)

Rumours (Ontario, Canada)

Rumours of Fleetwood Mac (Birmingham, England)

Rumours of Fleetwood Mac (Liverpool, England)

Food Fighters

Food Finders

Gratis Bier (3-mans Allround
coverband uit Leeuwarden)

Green Daze

Green-ish Day

Greener Day

Guns 'N Rozes

Guns 2 Roses

Gunz 'N 'F 'N Rosez

Guns N FN Roses

Guns Cover Brazil

Rocket Queen (A tribute to Guns
'n Roses—including tattoos—
featuring Blaxl Rose)

Rocket Queen (Los Angeles, CA;
"including tattoos, and without
needing any silly wigs . . .")

Rocket Queens ("NOT a G'n R
Tribute but a Tribute to Appetite
For Destruction only.")

Appetite For Destruction
(New York, NY; "Has opened twice
for Gilby Clarke of Guns 'N Roses.")

Appetite For Destruction
(Winston-Salem, NC)

Appetite For Destruction
(Canada)

Appetite For Deception

Rocket Queens (Pleasanton, CA)

Rocket Queen (Milan, Italy)

Hollywood Rose (Budapest,
Hungary)

Hollywood Rose (St. John's,
Newfoundland)

Hollywood Rose (Rome, Italy)

Hollywood Rose (Belgrade, Serbia)

Hollywood Roses (Los Angeles, CA)

Appetite For Illusion

Lose Your Illusion

Lines 'N Noses

Li'l GNR (first ever all-kids
tribute band to Guns 'N Roses)

Stone Velvet Roses (tribute to
Guns 'N Roses, Stone Temple Pilots,
and Velvet Revolver)

Area 51 (tribute to Guns 'N Roses
and Blind Faith; Vercelli, Italy)

Heartless

Heart Brigade ("Heart fans will take notice of Heart Brigade.")

Heart Love Alive

Dog N Butterfly ("In the world of tribute bands, the fans cried out, 'Will there ever be a good Heart tribute?'")

Iron Priest (tribute to Iron Maiden and Judas Priest)

Ironically Maiden

The Jamm

The Underground Jam

The Gift (featuring The Jam's drummer Rick Buckler)

The New Age Jam

Retro Tull

Living in the Past (a Jethro Tull tribute)

Aqualung (Los Angeles, CA)

Aqualung (Daytona Beach, FL)

Aqualung (Melbourne Beach, FL)

Locomotive Breath

Gimme Hendrix

Electric Lady

Rainbow Bridge

Ray's Rainbow Bridge

Are You Experienced

Fire

Crosstown Traffic

Randy Hansen: A Tribute to Jimi Hendrix (in blackface and out)

Rahmdee (Japan)

The Oreo Blue Experience

Jimi Jeff and the Gypsy Band

Electric Voodoo Child

Jimi's Image

The Hendrix Rockprophecy ("World's finest recitals of Jimi Hendrix music, from Michael Fairchild, the world's most widely read Hendrix scholar.")

A1A (Jimmy Buffet tribute)

Changes In Latitude

Margaritaville–Spirit of the Keys

Garratt & the Parrotheads

Live Bait

Departure (Journey)

Escape

Joy Revision

BRITISH STEEL
(JUDAS PRIEST TRIBUTE)

BRITISH STEEL
(ALBANY, NY)

BRITISH STEEL
(PORTLAND, NY)

JUDITH PRIEST (TEXAS,
ONLY FEMALE-FRONTED
JUDAS PRIEST TRIBUTE)

JUST AS PRIEST

JUSTICE PRIEST

JUST PRIEST

JUDAS BEAST

Kiss (Korean girl vocal trio; no relation to KISS)

Kisstroyer

Disstroyer

Kissteria

Akisstic (acoustic KISS tribute)

Kiss The Bride (husband and wife KISS Tribute duo; New Brunswick, Canada)

Kizz (Tokyo, Japan)

Kiss Dolls (Nagoya, Japan)

Neo Kiss (Nagasaki, Japan)

Torpedo Girl (all-girl tribute band; Tokyo, Japan)

The Torpedo Girls (Germany; unlike most tribute bands, the male band members wear no makeup or costumes while the two female background vocalists sport Ace's and Paul's makeup)

Smooch (all-girl tribute band; Toronto, Canada)

Kyss (Sweden)

Unmasked (Sweden)

Kiss This (England)

Kisstory (Sao Paulo, Brazil)

Kissed (Germany)

Kissed (Missouri)

Kist

Kiss'd

Kiss n' Tell

Kissa (Japan)

Kissology

Kissntell

Kiss Off

Kiss On The Rocks

KissKonfusion

Kissexy

Kisz (Bogota, Columbia)

Kisscovers

Kissteria

KissNation

Kisssexy (all girl)

Kiss My Ass

Kisser (Serbia)

Juliet Kiss (Verona, Italy)

Dynasty (Japan)

Dynasty (New Zealand)

Dynasty (Milwaukee, MN)

Dynissty (Australia)

Dressed to Kill (Ontario, Canada)

Dressed to Kill (England)

Dressed to Kill (New Jersey)

Dressed To Kiss (Rome, Italy)

Destroyer (Brazil)

Destroyer (Trondheim, Norway)

Destroyer (Ontario, Canada)

Destroyer (Portland, ME)

Destroyer (Houston, TX)

Strutter

Alive (Toronto, Canada)

Alive II (Nashville, TN)

Still Alive

Knights In SS

Knights In Satan's Service

Kings of the Nighttime World

Rip And Destroy

Psycho Circus

Starchild

SSIK (Austin, TX)

SSIK (Netherlands)

SSIK (Mexico)

Gods of Thunder

Phantoms of the Park

Love Gun (Puerto Rico)

Love Gun (Pennsylvania)

Detroit Rock City (Michigan)

War Machine

Black Diamond (Las Vegas, NV)

Black Diamond (Ohio; all-female)

Original Kiss Army

Larger Than Life (Germany; "KISS! That's all they dream about.")

Makin' Love (Japan; "We MAKIN' LOVE is some kinda promotion band of the KISS.")

Gene's Addiction (four band members dressed as Gene Simmons in a KISS Tribute)

Four Aces (four band members dressed as Ace Frehleys in a KISS Tribute)

Unmasked: A Magical Tribute To KISS ("Toronto Magician's KISS Tribute with the energy and attitude of a rock concert.")

Two Who Are One (a two-member tribute to Ace Frehley and Peter Criss; "We play at home . . .")

The Kissfits (A tribute to KISS and The Misfits)

Kentucky Kiss Tribute

The Paul Stanleys

Klown (KISS tribute with clown outfits and makeup)

She (all-female tribute to KISS; "Kiss With Tits")

Miss

Mini Kiss (all midget KISS tribute)

Tiny Kiss ("three midgets and one fat chick" KISS tribute)

The Australian Kiss Show

The Australian Ace Frehley Tribute Band

Klown ("The Largest Midget KISS Tribute Band In The World")

Kylie Likely

Led Zepplica

Lets Eppelin

Lets Zeppelin

Letz Zep

Led Zep Again

Led Zep Too

Lez Zeppelin (All Girls; All Zeppelin)

Mz. Led

Dread Zeppelin (Led Zeppelin done reggae style, with late-period Elvis-imitator Tortellvis)

Fred Zeppelin

Led Hed

Get The Led Out

Led On

Lets Zeppelin

Led Zepland

Led Blimpie

The Hindenburg Project

Graf Zeppelin

Led Heven (Temecula, CA)

Hammer of the Gods

Hammer of the Godz

Zepporama

Black Dog (Kitchener, ON)

BlackDog (Farmingdale, NY)

Black Dog (Stockton, UK)

Black Dog (Chula Vista, CA)

Black Dog (Clark, NJ)

Black Dog (DeMeern, Netherlands)

Zepparella (all-girl tribute)

The Song Remains The Same

Pure Meatloaf

Hot Summer Night

Meatloaf and Cher: The Ultimate Tribute

Limpish Biscuit

Absolute Madness

Utter Madness

Ultimate Madness

Complete Madness

Completely Mad

Badness

One Step Behind

The Madtones

Metalicish

Bill: Cleveland's Tribute to Metallica

Alcoholica

Damage Inc. (East Moline, IL)

Damage Inc. (São Paolo, Brazil)

Damage Inc. (Orange County, CA)

Damage Inc. (Greeley Hill, CA)

Damage Inc. (Rome, Italy)

Damage Inc. (Lindenhurst, NY)

Damage Inc. (Bridgeport, CT)

Damage Inc. (Beaver Falls, PA)

Bind and Purge

Mandonna (all-male Madonna tribute)

Lady Madonna

Move Over Madonna

The Cheeky Monkees

Little Crüe (midget Mötley Crüe tribute)

Live Wire (St. Paul, MN)

Live Wire (Portland, OR; "The only true Mötley Crüe tribute dressed in full shout at the devil outfits exactly!!!!!!! and no wigs!!!!!!!!")

Looks That Kill

Girls, Girls, Girls (all-girl Mötley Crüe)

HashiMötley Crüe (Japanese Mötley Crüe tribute)

Motorheadache

We're Not Motorhead

Hot Summer Night (Neil Diamond tribute)

Negative Creep (Nirvana tribute)

Teen Spirit

Lounge Act (Nirvana tribute)

Lithium (UK)

Lithium (US)

Demolution

Cobain

No Duh

Gwen In Doubt

OASISN'T

Damnation 101 (Glendale, CA)

Damnation 101 (Los Angeles, CA; "The drunkest Pantera Tribute.")

Sound Magazine (Partridge Family tribute)

Pink Voyd

Think Floyd

Pink Noise

Wish You Were Here (Cleveland, OH)

The Floydians

The Australian Pink Floyd Show

Dark Side of the Wall

Which One's Pink?

Just Floyd

Comfortably Numb

Floydian Slip

Polka Floyd (Toledo, OH)

Posin'

Look What the Cat Dragged In

Ratt Poison (tribute to Ratt, Poison, and the '80s)

Flesh&Blood

Flesh And Blood

The Secret Police

Ghost in the Machine

Stingchronicity

The Pretend Pretenders

Purple Reign

Perple Rain (Milwaukee's only Prince tribute band)

Purple Rain (UK)

Glam Slam (Norway)

Kween (Japan)

Almost Queen

Queer (Sweden)

QE II

The Bohemians

Killer Queen

God Save Queen

Everqueen

Kings of Queen

Gaga

The Ramoniacs

The Ramoones

The Ramouns

The Cabrones

The Blitzcretins

1234

The Ram-Ons

The Ramainz (featuring Dee Dee Ramone
[R.I.P], Marky Ramone, C. J. Ramone of
the actual Ramones)

Rocket To Russia

Rockit To Russia

The Ramonettes (all-girl tribute)

Ramonas (London, England)

The Ramonas (California)

The Carbonas

Blitzcretins

Los Ramons

The Gabba Gabba Heys

Red Hot Tribute Peppers

Red Hot Chili Tribute

Red Hot Silli Feckers
(Bristol, UK)

Red Not Chili Peppers
(Portsmouth, UK)

The Red Hot Chili Bastards
(Amsterdam, Holland)

Mild Green Chilis

Ljute Papprichice
(Belgrade, Serbia)

Mother's Milk

---

r.e.fem (all-female tribute to R.E.M.)

Rapid Imitation Movement Stipe

The Buck Stipes Here

THE ROLLIN STONED

THE ROLLING STAINS

THE ROLLING TONES

THE ROLLING CLONES

ROCKS OFF

21ST CENTURY STONES

HOT ROCKS

GIMME SHELTER

JUMPIN' JACK FLASH

STONED AGAIN

MIDNIGHT RAMBLERS

Anthem ("Arizona's tribute to Rush.")

Anthem (Tucson, AZ)

Anthem of Sacramento

La Vida Santana

The Sex Pistols Experience ("The world's leading & only worthwhile tribute show to one of the most influential bands of all time, featuring Johnny Forgotten, Steve Clones, Paul Crook, and Kid Vicious")

The Next Pistols

Es-sex Pistols (UK)

Never Mind The Trossachs

TransSexPistols ("Hollywood Cross dressing Sex Pistols Tribute;" formerly Pretty Vacant, non-cross dressing Sex Pistols Tribute)

No Future

Shania's Twin, featuring Carla Ouzas (Ontario, Canada)

Twain's Twin (Ontario, Canada)

Sharia Twain, featuring Shari Pascoe (Ontario, Canada)

The Shania Show (Ontario, Canada)

Superbly Shania (British Columbia, Canada)

Simply Shania (Edison, NJ)

Surely Bassey

The Sisters of Murphy
(The Sisters of Mercy tribute)

Slyde

Flamin' Slade

The Spicey Girls

STATE OF QUO

STATUS QUID

STATUS QUOTE

PRO QUID QUO

FAKE US QUO

STAID AS QUO

The Danny Steel Orchestra
(Steely Dan tribute, UK)

Pretzel Logic

The Royal Scam

Countdown To Ecstasy

Doctor Wu

Kid Charlemagne

The Clone Roses

Sublame

Second Hand Smoke (Chicago, IL)

Second Hand Smoke (Raleigh, NC)

Badfish

Forty Ounces

Wrong Way

Fat Lizzy
(a Thin Lizzy tribute)

Twin Lizzy

Tin Lizzy

Tinn Lizzy

Think Lizzy

Dizzy Lizzy

Limehouse Lizzy

The Bastard Sons of the Nuge

114

Petty Theft (a Tom Petty and the Heartbreakers tribute)

We B 40
UB Forte

Toto Recall

Practically Hip

Even Better Than The Real Thing—A Tribute to U2

Zoo2 (Chicago, IL)

Zoo2 (San Diego, CA)

ZU2 (Nottinghamshire, England)

U2 -Zoo (Cleveland, OH)

U2-Zoo (Spartanburg, SC)

Trib-U

2-U

U2-II

Us4

U2-UK

Exit—All Girl Tribute to U2
("as mentioned in Playboy . . .")

Rattle And Hum

Even Wetter
(Wet Wet Wet tribute)

Fan Halen

VH

Hot For Teacher (Los Angeles, CA)

Hot For Teacher (San Francisco, CA)

Hot For Teacher (Concepcion, Chile)

Diver Down

The Atomic Punks

Van Heaven

InHalen

X Halen

Lite Snake
(Worthing, UK)

Lite Snake
(Kent, UK)

ZZ Topped

ZZ Stop

BOTH KINDS OF MUSIC:
COUNTRY AND WESTERN

Good old country music has never been what it used to be. Ask anybody who cares. And several do. For example, a lot of pedal steel players, among them me, feel like they could be working more. And a lot of fiddle players feel like the pedal steel players are soaking up valuable fiddle time. As for what banjo pickers think . . . well, nobody gives much of a damn.

But country music is built on true tradition, much of it very creatively made up right on the spot. And the same goes for country band names. Once the early scratchy sounds of Skillet Lickers and Possum Hunters receded into the radio ether, in came a long-lasting vogue for names that suggested that those colorfully clad bronco-bustin', cattle-ropin' cowpokes up there on the stage might well be headed for the hills of Hollywood, where Driftin' Cowboys and Saddle Kings hunkered down and harmonized around authentic movie studio campfires.

But once the Western passed away (in 1939, 1949, 1959, 1969, or 1970, depending on when your dad and grandad quit going to the movies), the trend in country band names veered away toward the style generally known amongst hillbilly scholars as "Jim Bob Chart-Topper and the Song Hits." This trend continued unabated until Nashville, the Antichrist's own adopted hometown, had country music spayed, neutered, and put up for adoption. As a result, I'm sorry to say, there is actually a country band called Rascal Flatts. Sorry, buckaroos, but that's exactly where we draw the line.

The Sons of the Pioneers

The Sons of the Golden West

The Riders of the Purple Sage

The New Riders of the Purple Sage

Bob Manning and His Riders of the Silvery Sage

The Sons of the Sage

The Sons of the Range

The Sons of the Soil

The Sons of the West

Riders in the Sky

Hank Williams and the Drifting Cowboys

Gid Tanner's Skillet Lickers

Dr. Humphrey Bates and The Possum Hunters

Warmack's Gully Jumpers

The Fruit Jar Drinkers

The Tarheel Rattlers

The Binkley Brothers' Dixie Clodhoppers

Scotty Stevens and His Edmonton Eskimos

West Virginia Sweethearts

West Virginia Snakehunters

Cousin Ebb and His Ozark Squirrel Shooters

The Beverly Hillbillies

Dallas Boyd and the Musical Farmers

Roy Acuff and The Smoky Mountain Boys (formerly The Tennessee Crackerjacks, then The Crazy Tennesseans)

Johnny Cash and The Tennessee Two (later Johnny Cash and The Tennessee Three)

Noel Boggs

Blind Arthur Blake (Western & metropolitan...) and the boot sleepers

Betty and Her
Hillbilly Buddies

Rhonda Vincent
and The Rage

and The Rage

Hank Thompson and
the Brazos Valley Boys

Milton Brown and His
Musical Brownies

Adolph Hofner and
The Pearl Wranglers

Happy Fats Le Blanc
and his Rayne-Bo Ramblers

Texas Jim Trimble and His Stump Jumpers

Tiny Thomas and His June Tanglers

Big Bob Shafer and His Saddle Pals

Deacon Wayne and his Happy Hollow Cowboys

Paul (Hank) Preston and His White Mountaineens

Merle Lindsay and the Oklahoma Night Riders

Bob Pressley and His Sagebrush Serenaders

Waite's Pokeberry Promenaders

Billye Gale and the Hollywood Cowgirls

Dolly Parton
and the Family Band

Porter Wagoner
and the Wagonmasters

Merle Haggard
and the Strangers

Buck Owens and
the Buckaroos

Wanda Jackson
and the Party Timers
Loretta Lynn and the Coal Miners
Freddie Hart and the Heartbeats
Carl Smith and the
Tunesmiths

Bill Monroe and the Bluegrass Boys

Hank Snow and the Rainbow Ranch Boys

Flatt and Scruggs and the Foggy Mountain Boys

The Smoggy Mountain Boys

Homer Spangler and the Hocking Valley Boys

Gene Autry and the Pinafores

Faron Young and the Country Deputies

Ernest Tubb and the Texas Troubadours

The Texas Tornadoes

Rascal Flatts

Sawyer Brown

Alabama

Willie Nelson & Friends
(originally Willie Nelson and The Offenders, then Willie Nelson and the Record Men, later Willie Nelson & Family)

The Blue Sky Boys

The Oak Ridge Quartet
(later the Oak Ridge Boys)

Hylo Brown and the Timberliners

Sid King and The Five Strings

Waylon Jennings and the Waylors

Homer & Jethro

Lonzo & Oscar

Karl & Harty

Jim & Jesse

Reno & Smiley

Rusty & Doug

Buddy & Bob

Mac & Bob

Ezra & Elton

Brooks & Dunn

Big & Rich

Pappy, Zeke, Ezra & Elton

Tom, Dick and Harry

Marvin Rainwater

Mainer's Mountaineers

The East Texas Serenaders

Lulu Belle and Scotty

The Maddox Brothers and Rose (no relation to the Cornelius brother and sister Rose)

The Delmore Brothers

The Stanley Brothers

The Louvin Brothers

The Statler Brothers

The Osbourne Brothers

The Flying Burrito Brothers

The Acorn Sisters

The Stoneman Family

The Carter Family

The Massey Family

The Judds

The Prisonaires (Tennessee State Penal Institution)

The Radio Rangers

The Radio Rangerettes

The Radio Ranch Pals

The Radio Wranglers

The Radioaires

Ralph and Ruth and
the Radio Ramblers

Frank and Esther, the
Sweethearts of Radio

The Radio Ranch
Straight Shooters

The Range Riders

The Range Drifters

The Lazy Ranch Boys

The Easy Riders

The Les Paul Trio

Conway Twitty and The
Twitty Birds

The Blue Ridge Playboys
(with Floyd Tillman)

The Swift Jewel
Cowboys

Bob Biddle and
His Buckaroos

Johnny Western

Sheb Wooley and the
Purple People Eaters

Ray Price and the
Cherokee Cowboys

Webb Pierce and the
Wondering Boys

Pee Wee King and the
Golden West Cowboys

Wilma Lee and Stoney
Cooper and the Clinch
Mountain Clan

Miss Gene Campbell
and Her All Girl
Accordion Band

Ace Bailey and His
Utah Trailers

Al Hopkins and His
Buckle Busters

The Songfellows

Wagon Wheel
Ranch Boys

The Drifting
Mountain Boys

The Smilin' Hillbillies

The Dude Ranch
Buckaroos

The Korn Kobblers

The Komedy Kowboys

The Korn Krackers

The Alabama
Washboard Stompers

Lonesome Buddy

Lonesome Lloyd

Lonesome Shorty

Lonesome Valley Sally

Lonesome George and
the Eubanks Brothers

Patty Lu and the
Texas Sweethearts

The Beaver Valley
Sweethearts

Mary Lynne and the
Country Two Plus Three
(later the Gallileans)

Al and His Pals

Widow Smithers
and Sadie

The Toothless Twins

The Banjo Maniacs

The Buckskin Boys

Henry Ade and
His Stardusters

Jerry Byrd and His
Stringdusters

Jim Cook and the
Stringdusters

Claude Casey and
the Sagedusters

Betty Amos and
the Lump Boys

Eddie Arnold and His
Tennessee Plowboys

Uncle Rufe Armstrong
and His Coon Hunters

The Fiddlin' Bear Cats

Dean Armstrong and His
Arizona Dance Band

The Santa Fe
Trail Blazers

The Nitty Gritty
Dirt Band

Asleep At The Wheel

The Dixie Chicks

Trick Pony

Lady Antebellum

Little Big Town

Shenandoah

Highway 101

BR549

Cowboy Crush

Restless Heart

Sugarland

Little Texas

Nickel Creek

Hot Apple Pie

The Tractors

The Wreckers

The Mavericks

BlackHawk

Confederate Railroad

Forty5 South

Halfway to Hazard

Lone Star

The Grascals

Cross Canadian Ragweed

Southern Pacific

Wylie & the Wild West

McBride & The Ride

Montgomery Gentry

Diamond Rio

Dwight Yoakam and the
Babylonian Cowboys

Tim McGraw and the
Dancehall Doctors

Hank Caldwell and the
Saddle Kings

Jimmie Dale and His
Prides of the Prairie

The Pals of the Range

Three Prairie Daisies

She-Daisy

Al Rawley and His
Wild Azaleas

The Tumbleweed Twins

The Tolar Brothers and
Their Trail Riders

Cliff Godard's Reno
Racketeers

Hardrock Gunter and
the Thunderbirds

Dusty Dawson and His
Swingbillies

Sonny Day and His
Radio Raskals

Cowboy Em and His
Docey-Do Boys

Cowboy Loye

Cowboy Phil and the
Golden West Girls

Cowboy Sam

Cowboy Stuart

Cowboy Troy

Cowboy Slim Rinehart

Cowboy Donn Reynolds
and His T.V. Rangers

Jimmie Dale Gilmore and
the Continental Drifters

Cactus Slim The
Lonesome Serenader

Cowboy Tom and
Chief Shunatone

Cherokee Jack and the
Rhythm Ridin' Wranglers

Pie Plant Pete and
Bashful Harmonica Joe

The Cheery Sisters

Clem Gelewich and His
Happy Roamin' Rangers

Aunt Idy and
Uncle Juney

Cousin Emmy and
Her Kin Folk

THE MANY NAMES AND WONDROUS INCARNATIONS OF ELVIS

You probably don't want to name your band Elvis Presley because ASCAP, or SoundScan, or Lisa Marie Presley, or any combo thereof might get all up in your business, but maybe you can fool a few die-hard fans into downloading your first single by naming your all-percussion-all-of-the-time combo after one of Elvis' movie characters. That's right. Elvis wasn't just some moderately successful singer who pushed along the early jalopy of country and rhythm and blues; he was also the star of thirty-one films in the 1950s and '60s that anybody who called themselves a critic hated, but that millions of other potentially less-discerning people loved, or at least paid some money to see. Smartest of all were the producers who decided that whether Elvis was a former jailbird or a former trapeze artist, he was gonna sing for his supper.

CLINT RENO
(A COUNTRY BOY BACK
FROM THE CIVIL WAR)

VINCE EDWARDS
(A JAILBIRD TURNED
POP SINGER)

DEKE RIVERS
(A SMALL TOWN COUNTRY
BOY TURNED POP SINGER)

DANNY FISHER
(A CRIMINAL TURNED
NIGHTCLUB SINGER)

TULSA MCLEAN
(A TANK GUNNER TURNED
NIGHT CLUB SINGER)

PACER BURTON
(A HALF-BREED WARRIOR)

CHAD GATES
(A G.I. TURNED TOURIST GUIDE)

GLEN TYLER
(A SMALL TOWN COUNTRY BOY
JAILBIRD TURNED WRITER)

ROSS CARPENTER
(A FISHING GUIDE
TURNED SINGER)

TOBY KWIMPER
(A HILLBILLY FISHERMAN)

WALTER GULICK
(A BOXER TURNED CAR
MECHANIC)

MIKE WINDGREN
(A FORMER TRAPEZE ARTIST
TURNED LIFEGUARD AND
NIGHTCLUB SINGER)

MIKE EDWARDS
(A CROP-DUSTER PILOT
TURNED SMUGGLER)

JOSH MORGAN/JODIE TATUM
(AN AIR FORCE OFFICER/A
SMALL TOWN COUNTRY BOY)

CHARLIE ROGERS
(A SINGER TURNED CARNY)

LUCKY JACKSON
(A RACE CAR DRIVER)

RUSTY WELLS
(A POP SINGER TURNED GIRLS'
SCHOOL CHAPERONE)

JOHNNY TYRONE
(A MOVIE STAR TURNED ASSASSIN)

RICK RICHARDS
(A HELICOPTER PILOT)

LONNIE BEALE
(A FEMALE HEALTH
RANCH WRANGLER)

JOHNNY
(A MISSISSIPPI RIVERBOAT
GAMBLER)

MIKE MCCOY
(A RACE CAR DRIVER)

SCOTT HAYWARD
(A MILLIONAIRE TURNED
WATERSKI INSTRUCTOR)

GUY LAMBERT
(A POP SINGER)

TED JACKSON
(A NAVY FROGMAN)

GREG NOLAN
(A FREELANCE PHOTOGRAPHER)

STEVE GRAYSON
(A RACE CAR DRIVER)

JOE LIGHTCLOUD
(A HALF-BREED)

JESS WADE
(AN OUTLAW GONE STRAIGHT)

WALTER HALE
(A SHOW BUSINESS MANAGER)

JOHN CARPENTER
(A GHETTO DOCTOR)

lor Me Badd

You may succumb to the black urge to colorize your band's name. We can't stop you, of course, and wouldn't really try. We have better things to do. We're rehearsing and recording demos and trying to paint pinstripes on this Korean-made Strat copy we bought on eBay even though the neck sort of sucks, and, well, we feel like it's none of our damn business what you call your lame-ass band. But try to resist putting the name of a color in the name of your band, anyway. Plus, we've already copyrighted "Blue Floyd," so you can just forget about that one.

Pink Floyd

Frijid Pink

Pink Lady

Pink Martini

Mother Tucker's Yellow Duck

Red Noise

RED

Green Lyte Sunday

The Tangerine Zoo

Moby Grape

Tangerine Dream

Agent Orange

The Red Krayola

The Hydraulic Peach

The Lemon Pipers

Blue Cheer

The Screaming Blue Messiahs

The Blue Devils

The Blue Things

The Blue Boys

The Blue Velvets

The Blue Spots

Blue Sun

Clear Blue Sky

The Blue Sky Boys

The Bluebells

Patti LaBelle and the Bluebells (later LaBelle)

Black Sabbath

Black Flag

The Black Velvet Band

The Black Dyke Band

Black 47

Anus of a Black Cat

Black Rebel Motorcycle Club

Johnny Greene and the Green Men

Billy Lee Riley and the Little Green Men

Green Day

Green River

Golden Earring

Goldfrapp

The Golden Pharoahs

The Golden Palominos

The Golden Chords

Arthur J. and the Goldcups

Li'l Band of Gold

The Silver Beatles

The Silver Apples

The Silver Jews

The Silvertones

Silvertone

Yellow Magic Orchestra

Yello

Mustard Men

Mustard Plug

Cranberry Moustache

The Orchids

The Rhythm Orchids

Eve's Plum

The Pink Fairies

Dave McArtney and the Pink Flamingos

The Red, White, and Blues Band

Savoy Brown

The Browns

The Emeralds

Ruby

Shocking Blue

Blue Öyster Cult

Black n' Blue

The Black Diamonds

The Black Sorrows

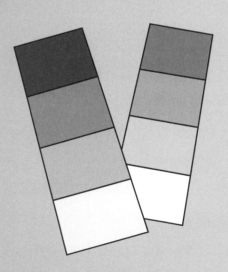

The Black Crowes

The Black Keys

The White Stripes

The White Knights

The Whites

White Lion

Whitesnake

Great White

The Average White Band

White Zombie

Soft White Underbelly

Plain White T's

Grey Matter

The Greys

The Pastels

Deep Purple

The Purple Hearts

The Purple Gang

The Lavender Hill Mob

Colourfield

Paul Kelly and the Coloured Girls
(slightly later, before first American tour,
Paul Kelly and the Messengers)

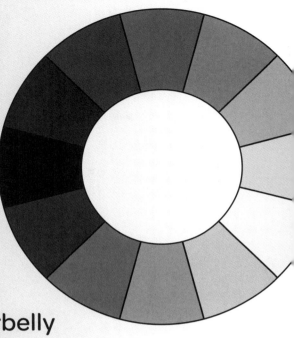

The Daughters of Eve

Well, in the heat of our loud, loud, loud rehearsals, Kathy would turn to her amp, to sip her tea, or dig in her purse puddled upon the amp, and that hollow body Hofner would start to feedback, building from a low hmmm, building, building, HMMMM, building, HHHMMMMMWHOOOOEEEEEEE, whereupon Debbie and I would yell "Kathy! Don't!"

We were, at that time, looking for a name, using the age-old practice of anything that came to mind. For example: the Three-Piece Power Trio, the Ass Kickers, the Drip Coffee Cones, the Loofas, the Car Keys, the Left Turn Indicators, the I Can't Park Here It's Illegal I'll Get A Ticket Oh Fuck It I'm Immortals, etcetera, the Etceteras. Etcetera. "Etcetera," a Celtic Metal band. Lots of dry ice . . .

It was maddening.

"Kathy! Don't!!"

"The Contractions?"

Lots of laughter. "Kathy Don't, Debbie Doesn't, Mary Won't!" Haw, haw, haw. Tee hee. Giggle. Giggle.

At that very moment, another musician opened the door to our room, and said, "You guys sound good, what's your name?"

We looked at each other, and answered, "The Contractions."

Tada.

— *Mary Kelley, guitarist, songwriter for San Francisco's truly, genuinely great all-woman trio, The Contractions. They were astonishing and amazing and adventurous in the early '80s, and are now playing once again. Miss 'em only if you dare.*

The Girls

The Spice Girls

All Girl Summer
Fun Band

Girlband

Slumber Party Girls

Twelve Girls Band

Two Nice Girls

The All-Girl Boys

All Angels

All Saints

Girls Aloud

Girlschool (formerly
Painted Lady)

The Catholic Girls

American Girls

The Indigo Girls

Sex Bomb Girls

The GTOs (Girls Together
Outrageously)

Girl In A Coma

Instant Girl

eX-Girl

Girl Monster

Everything But The Girl

Anything But Monday

Spitboy

The Runaways

Christian! Teenage Runaways

The Slits

Slant 6

The Chicks

The Chic-lets

Chicks on Speed

The Dixie Chicks

Dickless

Halfcocked

Fanny *(previously The Svelts)*

Birtha

Wilma

Zelda

Isis

She *(formerly The Hairem)*

S.H.E.

Shesus

The Belle Stars

Bellefire

Bellepop

The Deadly Nightshade *(formerly The Moppets)*

POW *(Pride of Women)*

Antigone Rising

The Carrie Nations

The Glamazons

Waking The Witch

Bitch

Bitch Alert

7 Year Bitch

Bitch Fight

16 Bitch Pile-Up

Rockbitch

The Ping Pong Bitches

The Pixies 3

The Chubbies

Chubby Bunny

Huggy Bear

The Dolls

The Demures

The Honeys

The Popsicles

The Cupcakes

The Cookies

The Jelly Beans

Lollipop

Sugarbabes

Sugar and the Spice

Goldie and the Gingerbreads

Ginger and the Snaps

Candy and the Kisses

The Treacle People

The Joy of Cooking

Sweet Female Attitude

The Bittersweets

Candy Ass

Cake Like

The Cake

Cheesecake

Kathy Lynn and the Playboys

The Pinups

The Cheerleaders

The Majorettes

The Playgirls

The Paper Dolls

Bombshells

The Good Girls

The Stepping Stones

Porcelain and the Tramps

The Wives

The Bags

The Bangs

The Bangles

The Bootles

The Beatle-ettes

The Beatle Buddies

The Liver Birds

The Braillettes

Connie and the Cones

Siouxsie and the Banshees

Switchblade Kittens

Atomic Kitten

Josie and the Pussycats

Kittie

Bad Kitty

The Applicators

Barbarella

The Be Good Tanyas

The Pandoras

Paula and the Pandoras

Judi Johnson and
the Perfections

Jessica James and
the Outlaws

Lulu and the Luvvers

Lorraine and the Socialites

The Royal Debs

The Z-Debs

Mama Lion

Tiger Trap

Tiger Lily
(formerly The Tomboys,
The Cat Women)

Indavana Bluz

Ramatam

The Ace of Cups

The Trans-Sisters

Transvision Vamp

The Tammys

The Tom Boys

The Murmaids

The Masterettes

The Fashionettes

The Flirtations

The Exciters

The Rev-Lons

The Whyte Boots

The Nu Luvs

The Reginas

Feminine Complex

The Prissteens

Heavens to Betsy

Hey Girl!

The Holograms

New Haven Women's
Liberation Rock Band

The Women's Philharmonic

The Poison Girl Band

Toxic Lipstick

Mythika

MaRioNettE

Mis-Teeq

Sobriquet

Spanking Machine

The Wailin' Jennies

Bratmobile

Puffy Ami Yumi

Cibo Matto

Cindy Loo Whos

Cougar Party

Crucified Barbara

Dolly Mixture

Dusty Trails

Go Betty Go

The Go-Go's

The Mo-Dettes

OOIOO

Growing Up Skipper

Gidget Goes To Buffalo

Princess Princess

Mustang Sally

The Iron Maidens

Jack The Lass

Lez Zeppelin

The Ramonas

Cheap Chick

PMS
(Pre Metal Syndrome)

The Menstrual Tramps

Mourning Sickness

The Murmurs

Pink Champagne

Plain Jane

Scissor Girls

Some Girls

Super Monkey

Super Junkie Monkey

Spreens

Tegan and Sara

The Topp Twins

Venus Envy

The Veronicas

Vixen

The Violents

The Z-Rays

The Astronettes

Sugar Crush

The Pipettes

Morning Musume

Country Musume

Kleenex (litigation, then Liliput)

The Rezillos

The Revillos

Castration Squad

The Daughters of Eve

The Pleasure Seekers

Carol Bennett and the Satisfiers

The Violents

The Hissyfits

The Screamin' Sirens

Throwing Muses

Belly

Feline

Killer Pussy

Pussy Face

Pussy Galore

Ladytron

The Lame Flames

Sheraw

Vixen

Venus and The Razorblades

Babes In Toyland

The Butchies

LeTigre

The Breeders

Boss Hog

Veruca Salt

Cameltoe

Team Dresch

Sleater-Kinney

Cycle Sluts From Hell

Mary's Danish

Elastica

The Gits

The Female Chauvinist Pigs

The Plasmatics

The Genitorturers

Venus Flytrap

Bratmobile

Frightwig

Fluffy

The Gore Gore Girls

Rachel and the Revolvers

Regina and the Redheads

Ruby and the Romantics

Rosy and the Originals

Patti Lace and the Petticoats

Heart

The Heathertones

Mediaeval Baebes

The Merry Wives of Windsor

Jack Off Jill

Klymaxx

A Taste of Honey

Sweet Honey in the Rock

Honeycomb

54 Nude Honeys

Luscious Jackson

Precious Metal

The Trashwomen

The Count Backwards

The Glamour Pussies

The Pussycat Dolls

Robin Lane and the
Chartbusters

Linda Lane and the Sinners

Melinda and the Misfits

Tina and the Mexicans

Holly and the Italians

Terry and the Tunisians

Tracy and the Plastics

Shelly Shoop and the
Shakers

Barbara Allen and the
Tennessee Hot Pants

Pink Lady (later Pink
Lady and Jeff)

Prettier Than Pink

Shonen Knife

Live Nude Girls

The Ikettes

Roxette

The Shaggs

The Roches

The Braxtons

The Boswell Sisters

The Andrews Sisters

The King Sisters

The Lennon Sisters

The DeCarlo Sisters

The Gee Sisters

The Capri Sisters

The Half Sisters

The Android Sisters

The Silver Sisters

The Star Sisters

The Sisters

The Soul Sisters

The Sledge Sisters
(later Sister Sledge)

Little Sister (earlier The Stone Sisters, later Sister Stone)

The Pointer Sisters

The Paris Sisters

The Pfister Sisters

The Fontane Sisters

The Scissor Sisters

The Sisters of Mercy

The Sisters of Murphy

Shakespeare's Sister

Uncle Earl

The Nuns

The Singing Nun

Romeo Void

Anti-Scrunti Faction

Bananarama

Salt -N- Pepa

Mel & Kim

Pepsi & Shirley

Carol and Cheryl

The Topp Twins

The Pierces

SWV (Sisters With Voices)

ESG

TLC

Oaktown 357

En Vogue

The Mamas & The Papas

The Emotions

The Three Degrees

Appolonia 6

The Mary Jane Girls

The Cheetah Girls

Bardot

Hepburn

The Gonnnabes

The Jaynettes

Las Ketchup

SheDaisy

Betty

The Veronicas

Wendy and Lisa

The Wreckers

Teen Idol names

In a far away land, long ago, way, way before *High School Musical 1, 2,* or *3,* or even before the Jurassic era of NKOTB, there were young men who had only modicums of talent and were adored and screamed at by young women who didn't care. That transitional time between *really* loving horses and studying for the American Her-Story 101 midterm at Wellesley was a weird and wonderful time of platonic sexuality that wasn't marred by anything icky (well, there was that Gary Glittery stuff, but that was way later), and a cute boy with nice hair was just about the most important thing. Ever.

wee willie harris

lonnie donnegan

tommy steele

marty wilde

billy fury

johnny gentle

T. J.

vince eager

duffy power

dickie pride

rory storm

adam faith

georgie fame

cliff richard

pat boone

johnny kidd and the pirates

leapy lee

tommy quickly

vince taylor

joe meek

jimmy justice and the excheckers

(band members formerly of emile ford's checkmates)

tom jones

engelbert humperdinck

gilbert o'sullivan

gary glitter

alvin stardust

EH 4ever!

I ♡ P.B.

153

Keep It Short, Stupid

Short is sweet. And the shorter the band name, the bigger the letters on the poster can be. Plus, there's the painful issue of band logo tattoos. Think about it. (But somebody already used "It," so don't.)

KISS
YES
IF
A
E
I
O
U
U2
UK
FM
ZED

(NOTE: THE THE WAS CONSIDERED FOR THIS SECTION BUT REJECTED AS TOO REDUNDANT.)

ALL BE
US, ETC.
UP
UPP
CARP
CAN
CUB

SKY

SKYY

THE SKY
(DISQUALIFIED)

AIR

FOG

FIRE

JAE

TRAIN

TRUK

SUB

THE

X

THE EX

WAR

RAGE

PUSH

TANK

ZAPP

NUTZ

RIDE

RATT

FAT

FAG

DIO

THEM

THIS

RUSH

LIVE

LIFE

FEAR

BUSH

GO

GOO

GOB

GONG GUN

KORN

KRANK

CHROME

CROW

BIRD

EGG

CRACK

KAK

TIME

LIFE

DEATH

FREE

STORM

SOIL

FYRE

ICE

FOG

SMOKE

ASH

ARK

ARCH

BLUR

BITCH

BUX

FANG

WIG

WILD

CLAW

OWL

DUCK

CHASE

WEEN

STYX

KIX

FOX

LAMB

DEUCE

TASTE

TOOL

TUFF

PAN

PAX

PRIDE

PROOF

SAGE

SEX

SONG
(FEATURING
MICKEY
ROONEY, JR.)

MU
(FORMERLY
OF THE
IMPACTS,
THE EXILES,
CAPTAIN
BEEFHEART
AND THE
MAGIC BAND)

OM

MUD

PUD
(LATER
THE DOOBIE
BROTHERS)

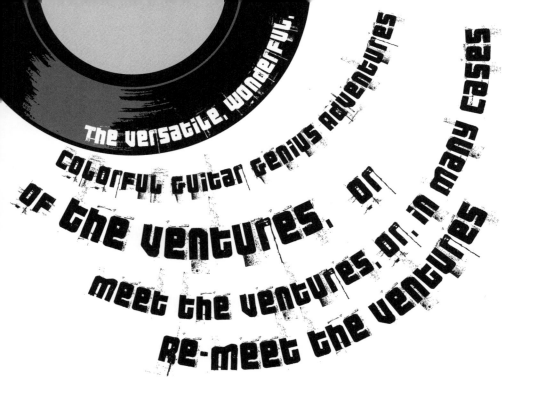

The versatile, wonderful,
colorful guitar genius adventures
of the Ventures, or
meet the Ventures, or, in many cases
re-meet the Ventures

And here I commend to your attention not an entire genre, or even an entire band name genre, but simply the sacred name of a single band, a band older even than the Rolling Stones, and longer lasting, with pretty much about the same number of personnel changes.

The Ventures provide us a profound and powerful lesson. The band's career, lasting forty-plus-odd years or so thus far, has been based entirely on the verities. Most of all, and above all, and beyond all: Don't Change Your Name Once You Get Famous.

Oh, and beyond all that, Don't Change Your Name: Change The Name Of Your Albums.

Duh.

And yet this simple principle has eluded 99.999% of all famous bands ever. I guess because there are just so many great possible names out there dangling like disco balls, spinning, shining, tantalizing you, luring you. Or worse, luring the drummer. Like when the Ventures' drummer Mel Taylor couldn't help but create Mel Taylor and the Magics—you can see how irresistible that could be.

I repeat: Don't change the name of your famous band; change the name of your album, change the color of the bikini on the curvaceous girl on the cover, change the brand of guitars you're totally associated with, change whatever style of music you're totally associated with, leap at, and on, and all over every new wave and nu-metal and new wave of heavy metal and every other cheesy trend, and frequently. You can change the very continent you sell records on (although Japan is certainly a better choice most years than Zimbabwe, as far as record purchase per capita goes, not to mention touring conditions) but just keep plugging, or plugging in. To whatever brand of guitar you're currently endorsing.

I mean, a band like Yes is sort of like the Ventures of the 1970s, in that they were, early on, however briefly it now seems as the decades spill past, associated with like a particular kind of sound that they spearheaded, sort of. And when things got a trifle thin in the early eighties, they went somewhat hip-hop techno pop. Esque. And got a big huge pop hit by doing so—sort of like when the Ventures had their second biggest hit ever maybe ten years into it with "Hawaii Five-O"—and so now if you go to a Yes show, you've got all these elderly geezers in the audience who want to hear early eighties hip-hop techno-pop nostalgia, and then a whole 'nother set of even more geezerly geezers who want to hear those bitchin' guitar instrumental changes—no, wait, that's the Ventures—or no, it could be like vintage Yes, too, I guess.

Or consider the Grateful Dead. I mean, once they found their somewhat-OK generic psychedelic-type name, they stuck with it, no matter what style—or in their case, shape—of music they were slappin' away at. (Although, since the Ventures were no longer calling themselves the Versatones, probably they could have just snagged that.) I mean, Jerry Garcia, the sorta musical guy in the band, after about four or five years of standing somewhere near the swirling center of the universe of undifferentiated pitch—and that was just when they were practicing vocal harmonies—finally went out and bought himself a double-neck, twenty-two-string pedal steel guitar with like eight pitch-shifting pedals and five pitch-shifting knee-levers too, no doubt figuring if he was going to float around in the vortexing cosmos of inadvertent modal chord-changing microtones, he might as well have the biggest gun on the block.

Well, as you do, once he got a pedal steel—or actually, like about an hour or two later, maybe—he started a country band, the New Riders of the Purple Sage, and they immediately commenced whacking away at country songs for like three hours or so in front of every Grateful Dead show. But He Didn't Quit His Famous Name Band, and even though the Grateful Dead sang country music every bit as good as they sang, say, blues, or R&B, or their own songs, or anything else with words or sounds attached to it, he didn't rename his famous band the New Riders, he just practiced pedal steel on three-chord country songs for like two or three hours on stage, and then he went back into the wailing world of wobbly tuning for another three or four hours.

Well, that stuff can be dangerous. Eventually you do heroin and smoke crack and die and so forth. And in mourning, your fellow Grateful Dead band dudes all dutifully agree that seeing as how things will never be the same, they'll never be known as the Grateful Dead again.

Big mistake, man. Huge mistake. I mean, you'd think they'd've checked in with the Ventures, who could have helped 'em out. I mean, pretty soon the biggest live act in the world was reduced to doing Grateful Dead tribute tunes under dopey names like Ratdog or the Other Ones. But time and economics heal all band-wounds, however briefly, and while they probably had some legal reason why they couldn't call themselves the Grateful Dead anymore, after much diplomacy and meetings on neutral corners near Haight and Ashbury, they settled on the super-catchy solution: the Dead. If you can't rake in big bucks with a name like that, you should probably just stay home and practice your ax, man. In private. With a strobe tuner.

The point being, as any Venturehead could have told you, keep The Name nice and safe, and solid, and intact. Hell, the more you change the album names (*Aoxomoxa, Live Dead, American Beauty, Workingman's Ventures, the Ventures Go Aozxomoxa Live, the Ventures Go To Heaven, Beauty! In Japan*) the more you get to have completely different album cover imagery, and that can only help the merch sales. Think skulls and skeletons, and then skulls and roses, and then dancing teddy bears, and then guns and roses and dancing guns and skulls, and guns and teddy bear skulls and dancing roses, and then slap a bunch of tie-dye over anything that doesn't sell quick. Either that, or girls in bikinis always work out good too. Ask the Ventures.

Walk Don't Run

The Ventures

Another Smash

The Colorful Ventures

Twist With The Ventures
(Dance)

Twist Party-Vol. 2 (Dance
with The Ventures)

Mashed Potatoes and Gravy
(Beach Party)

Going To The Ventures'
Dance Party

The Ventures Play Telstar
and Lonely Bull

Bobby Vee Meets The
Ventures

Surfing

The Ventures Play Country
Classics (I Walk the Line)

Let's Go!

The Ventures In Space

The Fabulous Ventures

Walk Don't Run, Vol. 2

Knock Me Out!

The Ventures In Japan

Caravan

The Ventures On Stage

The Ventures A Go-Go

The Christmas Album

The Ventures In Japan, Vol. 2

Adventures in Paradise
(aka The White Album)

The Trini Lopez Show
TV Special Soundtrack

Play Guitar With The
Ventures, Vol. 1–3

Play Electric With The
Ventures (Vol. 4)

Play Guitar With The Ventures
(Vol. 7) (Volumes 5 and 6 did not
actually include The Ventures)

Live in Japan 1965

Where The Action Is

Blue Sunset

The Ventures On Stage Encore

The Ventures Play the
Batman Theme

Go With The Ventures

Runnin' Strong

Wild Thing!

All About The Ventures Live

Guitar Freakout (later named
Revolving Sound; titled Guitar
Breakout in Japan)

Pops In Japan

Super Psychedelics (later Changing Times)

Ventures Deluxe

Wonderful Ventures

U.S. Navy Presents The Ventures

Golden Greats

Golden Original Hits

$1,000,000 Weekend (aka Groovin')

The Versatile Ventures

Guitar Genius of The Ventures

Live Again

Pops In Japan, No. 2

Pops Sound

Best of Surfing

The Ventures In Tokyo '68

Deluxe Double, Vol. 1

Flights Of Fantasy

The Horse (later On The Scene, also Ventures Today)

Underground Fire · Deluxe Double, Vol. 2 · Hawaii Five-O · This Is the Ventures, Vol. 1

House of the Rising Sun

Super Group

Journey To the Moon

Swamp Rock

More Golden Greats

Golden Pops

The Ventures Live

10th Anniversary Album

Best of The Ventures On Stage

A Decade With The Ventures

Best of Pop Sounds

Expo Seven-O

This Is The Ventures, Vol. 3

Best 20, Vol. 2

Pops In Japan '71

On Stage '71

Best 20, Vol. 3

Best 14

New Testament

Portrait

The Ventures Superpak

Theme From Shaft

Joy: The Ventures Play the Classics

The Ventures Play the Country Lovesick Blues

Rock and Roll Forever

Something Old, Something New

Golden Disc, Vol. 1

Golden Disc, Vol. 2

Golden Disc, Vol. 3

The Ventures On Stage '72

The Ventures On Stage '73

Pops In Japan '73

2001 (aka Only Hits)

The Jim Croce Songbook

The Ventures Play The Carpenters

15 Years of Japanese Pop

The Very Best of The Ventures

Now Playing

The Ventures On Stage '74

Rocky Road: The New Ventures

TV Themes

The Ventures On Stage '75

Hollywood: Yuya Uchida Meets The Ventures

All About The Ventures (three-record set)

Live In Korea

Best Now

Early Sounds

Pops In Japan, Vol. 1

Pops In Japan, Vol. 2

Pops In Japan, Vol. 3

The Ventures On Stage '76

Golden Double 32, Vol. 1

Golden Double 32, Vol. 2

Surfin' '77

Rock & Roll Graffiti

Live In Japan '77

Masters of Pop Music

Superdisc Golden Double

Deluxe In GoGo Beat

Deluxe In Rock Beat

Best Hits

The Ventures In Space '78

Surfin' USA '78

The Ventures On Stage '78

20 Greatest Hits

New Best 20

Rare Collection

Chameleon

Super Live '80

'60s Pop

The Collection: Ventures Forever

Pops In Japan '81

Tokyo Calling

KIKI Presents Ventures Big Hits

Japanese Graffiti

Soundtrack for "I Want To Marry A Woman" (aka The Ventures Meet The Tonics)

Latin Album

Greatest Hits, Vol. 1

NASA 25th Anniversary Commemorative Album (aka 25 Years in Space)

Radical Guitars

Rock & Roll Adventure

Guitar Power

In The Vaults

The Best Of The Ventures

Hits! Up To Date

St. Louis Memory

Last Album On Liberty

The Mosrite Years

The Fender Years

Surfin' Deluxe

The Japanese Melody

Movie Themes

Farewell Party: The Orange Sisters With The Ventures

Big Artist Flash: Greatest Hits

Walk Don't Run, Vol. 2

Stars On Guitars

Wild Again

The Ventures Play Southern All Stars (Southern All Stars were an '80s Japanese super group)

Live in Japan 1990

Best Now

Best of Live '65-69

The Ventures Play Seaside Story

The Ventures Play Major Motion Picture Themes

Bright Old Days

Best Now, Vol. 2

The Rarities

Melody Hits in Japan

Metal Dynamic Sound 3000

Best Hits By Request

Bel Age With the Ventures

Say Yes

Flyin' High

Live Twin Best

Den Deke Deke Deke

The Ventures Play Mega Hits

Golden Hits

Super Best Collection 25

Live in Japan 1993

Super Best, Vol. 1

Super Best, Vol. 2

Super Best, Vol. 3

Single Collection, Vols. 1-4

'93 In Japan

Cool Deluxe

Pops Ala Carte

Wild Again; The Ventures Play Heavy Hitters

Forever Fender

Wild Again II: Tribute to Mel Taylor

Unforgettable

Unbelievable

The Best Surfin' Hits

Wild Again Concert '97

V-Gold

Walk Don't Run 2000

MTV History 2000

The Ventures Play Runaway

Space 2001

Kayo Taizen (Cool Melody)

Super Best Hits

Pioneros Del Rock

The Very Best of The Ventures: Kayama Yuzo Selection

V-Gold II

Acoustic Rock

In Japan Live 2000

V-Gold III

The Ventures Play Southern All Stars —Tsunami

V-Gold Live II

'60s Rockin' Christmas

Surf Rock Anthology

Hyper V-Gold (aka V-Gold IV)

Live In Seattle, USA

Greatest Gold

Guitar Legends

Your Hit Parade '60s

In Japan Live 2002

V-Gold Blend: The Very Best of The Ventures

Summer and Winter Live

Classic Country Plus

New Depths (introducing The Rice Girls)

In the Vaults, Vol. 2

The Mel Taylor Memorial Collection

Supermow

The Ultimate Collection

Christmas Joy

Be Strong, America

Surfin' To Baja

Tele-Ventures

Only Hits

(Plus various solo albums from Mel Taylor and the Magics, Mel Taylor and the Dynamics, Nokie Edwards, Nokie Edwards and Ad-Venture, and Bob Spalding, The Fifth Venture.)

LOCATION, LOCATION, LOCATION

The great thing, the best thing, about a place like this would be getting the hell out of here, and soon. Man, what a hick town this one turned out to be! And the fact that we named our band after it has worked out to be a major mistake. What we should have done is what Berlin did, and Japan, and Billy J. Kramer and the Dakotas did. I mean, none of them had ever been to the places they named their bands after, but once they made records and stuff, they were almost guaranteed to be stars there. Which is why I'd like to kill our singer—well, it's one of the reasons I'd like to kill our singer. The name of the band was his idea. Who names their band after their hometown when their hometown is Hicksville?

THE OHIO PLAYERS

THE OHIO EXPRESS

THE OHIO UNTOUCHABLES

OHIO

THE DETROIT EMERALDS

DENNIS COFFEY AND THE DETROIT GUITAR BAND

**MITCH RYDER AND THE DETROIT WHEELS
(LATER KNOWN AS DETROIT)**

THE MEMPHIS HORNS

THE TIJUANA BRASS

THE BAJA MARIMBA BAND

THE MIAMI SOUND MACHINE

OZARK MOUNTAIN DAREDEVILS

THE GEORGIA SATELLITES

THE KENTUCKY HEADHUNTERS

THE OAK RIDGE BOYS

CHARLES WRIGHT AND THE WATTS 103RD STREET RHYTHM BAND

SERGIO MENDES & BRASIL '66 (PREVIOUSLY SERGIO MENDES & BRASIL '65, THE SERGIO MENDES TRIO, LATER SERGIO MENDES & BRASIL '77, SERGIO MENDES & THE NEW BRASIL '77)

SIR LORD BALTIMORE

BOBBY TAYLOR AND THE VANCOUVERS

RONNIE AND THE DAYTONAS

TONY ORLANDO AND DAWN

NASHVILLE PUSSY

THE NASHVILLE TEENS

THE NASHVILLE BLUEGRASS BAND

THE HOLLYWOOD ARGYLES

THE HOLLYWOOD CHICKS

THE HOLLYWOOD BRATS

FRANKIE GOES TO HOLLYWOOD

L.A. GUNS

YUKON

ALASKA!

MINNESOTA
(FORMERLY
COPPERHEAD)

NANTUCKET

VENICE
LOS ANGELES
CALEXICO

ATLANTA RHYTHM
SECTION

BLACK OAK ARKANSAS

PHOENIX

LITTLE TEXAS
TEXAS

THE UK SUBS
CHELSEA
DANZIG

BEIRUT
NAZARETH

MISSION OF
BURMA

HANOI ROCKS
(FINLAND)

TOKIO HOTEL
(GERMANY)

HIROSHIMA

SAIGON
KICKS

THE LITTLE RIVER BAND

THE ENGLISH BEAT

SQUEEZE UK

UK

BILLY J. KRAMER AND THE DAKOTAS

THE MERSEYBEATS

THE MERSEY BEATLES

LYNN AND THE MERSEY MAIDS

HATFIELD AND THE NORTH

TAMMY AND THE CAROLINAS

SLEATER-KINNEY

MANITOBA (LITIGATION, NOW CARIBOU)

RUSSIA (FROM SEATTLE)

OF MONTREAL (FROM ATHENS, GEORGIA)

EAST AFRICAN FAIR (FROM CANADA)

NORWAY (FROM NEW JERSEY)

BALTIMOORE (FROM SWEDEN)

BALCONES FAULT

HALIFAX (CALIFORNIA)

DISNEYLAND AFTER DARK

TEXAS IS THE REASON

ALCATRAZZ

EARTH

surf's out

Scholars largely agree that the earliest surf music was created when the gentle waves of the blue Pacific lapped against the hollow bamboo of the tiki bar—no, wait, that was lounge music. Surf music was invented when Southern California dudes who'd heard Mexican musicians faking flamenco runs realized that if you snagged that and then cranked the reverb tank on a Fender amp, you'd sound like God coming back from a beer run with glasspack mufflers on a big block Chevy. In a gravel parking lot. And it was good.

Link Wray and the Raymen

Dick Dale and the Del-Tones

Davie Allen and the Arrows

The Urban Surf Kings

Agent Orange

The Balboas

The Coastals

The Huntingtons

The Challengers

The Crowd (formerly The New)

The Aqua Velvets

Agent Orange

The Halibuts

Jon and the Nightriders

Los Straitjackets

The Del-Vamps

The Insect Surfers

The Illusions

The Crossfires (became The Turtles, then The Phlorescent Leech and Eddie, then Flo & Eddie)

Susan and the Surftones

The Mar-Kets

The Tornadoes

The Knights
The Lonely Knights
The Astronauts
Laika and the Cosmonauts
The Space Cossacks
The Aquamarines

The Reluctant Aquanauts   The Aquatones

The Shitones   The Raybeats   The Revels

Squid Vicious   The Volcanos   Thee Phantom Five

The Wet Suits   The Imperials

The Seamonkees   The Moon Monkeys

The Fantastic Baggys

Pollo Del Mar

The Pendletones

The Wet-Tones

The Phantom Surfers

The Penetrators

The Vibrocounts

The Woodies

The Surf Kings

The Diamondheads

The Bitch Boys

The Moon-Rays

The Lunar-Tikis

The Butthole Surfers

The Clams

The Sharkskins

Sublime

The Stingrays

The Aquajads

The Bikini Men

The Ziggens

The Slackmates

The Aquanettes

The Reverburritos

The Royaltones

The Sonics

Satan's Pilgrims

The Tikis

The Aquanautas

The Manatees

The Mermen

The Original Surfaris

The Treblemakers

Sharks   The Submersians

The Beach Nuts

Breakaways   The Beach Breaks

The Sonars   The Stallions

The Tuba   The Surf Suits   The Pipelines

Perdidos   The Torquays   The Mossrites   The Tikitones   The

Los   The Sir Finks   The Sandblasters   The Nebulas

The Surfaris   The Neptunas   The Nebulas

Because New Wave has always been such a stiff and sternly-defined genre, there are more rules than usual for inclusion here. A band (or maybe a solo artist, or a singer/songwriter who wasn't getting the job done in pub rock, country rock, folk, or sometimes a couple of guys who had nothing else to do, but there could be a girl, too) had to have an album (or an EP, or a single, or a 12-inch, or a cassette) released with a picture sleeve (or a picture disc) showing them with short hair (at least in front) and a perky or at least not too grumpy expression. If they wore a tie, it had to be skinny and not knotted too tightly, or else it had to be a bolo tie, but if more than one band member wore one, then you were a cowpunk band, which was still kind of new wave, but wasn't totally. And if you wore a suit jacket, the sleeves had to be pushed up. Or, you could be included if you had your record pressed in colored vinyl, as long as we don't count black as one of the colors. You could be power pop, or power pub, or dance pop, or no wave, or neo-rockabilly, or a few other things, but No Metal Allowed. Unless everybody cut their hair and wore stripy shirts. OK, so you could maybe have some members with long hair, but not all of them, unless you were the Ramones, or unless you talked the damn drummer into putting on a skinny tie or wearing a vest over his hairy, bare chest. And no bell-bottoms whatsoever. I don't care how hard it is to find a good drummer! Or at least make him wear a shirt with no sleeves and pink stripes. And pin some pink and orange badges on him. But that's it! After that, nobody else gets in! Period.

Blondie Talking Heads The
Modern Lovers The Rubinoos
The Action The Quick The Fast
The Knack The Know The Now
The Nice The Good The Most
The Pop The Go The Go-Go's
The Wet The Beat The English
Beat The Romantics The Motors
The Cars The Keys The Suburbs
The Yachts The Motels The
Holidays The Tours The Tourists
The Waitresses The Police The
Smirks The Shirts The Hooters
The Brains Mental As Anything
The Mumps The Mumbles The
Marbles The Singles The Records
The Hits The Hitmakers The
Payola$ The Cut-Outs The
Numbers The Low Numbers
The Stiffs The Bad Beats The
Bangs The Bangles The Bees
The Boys The Boyz The Boize
Just Boys The Cold The Chill
The Confidentials The
Continentals The Criminals
The Cryers The Lyres The

Explosions The Furys The Names
The Necessaries The Nervous
Eaters The News The Nines No
Sisters The Outlets The Outsets
The Rattlers The Rockin' Bricks
The Sneakers The Spongetones
The Trend The Tools The Spiffs
Trixy and the Testones The
Textones The Tunes The Zeros
The Wigs The Wackers Pete
Holly and The Looks The
Imposters The Distractions The
Contractions The Jumpers
The Favourites The Fabulous
Poodles The Boomtown Rats
The Lime Spiders The Flying
Lizards A Flock of Seagulls
Squeeze (from the UK) The Models
The Vibrators The Vapors The
Rich Kids The Plimsouls The Last
The Zippers The Psychedelic
Furs Tom Petty and The
Heartbreakers Split Enz Oingo
Boingo Devo The B-52s The Rezillos
The Revillos The Mysteroids
The Bongos The Go-Betweens

Wall of Voodoo

Siouxsie and the Banshees

Adam and the Ants

Katrina and the Waves

Jane Aire and the Belvederes

Bonnie Hayes and the Wild Combo

Bette Bright and The Illuminations

Martha and the Muffins

Venus and The Razorblades

Robin Lane and the Chartbusters

Jamie James and the Kingees

Roy Loney and the Phantom Movers

Flash and the Pan

Wang Chung

Soft Cell

The Human League

Orchestral Manoeuvres In The Dark

The DBs

The Fleshtones

The Feelies

The Individuals

Wreckless Eric

Elvis Costello

Elton Motello

Mink DeVille

Moon Martin

Joe Jackson

John Hiatt

Marshall Crenshaw

Steve Forbert

John Cooper Clarke

Curtiss A

The Paley Brothers

Donnie Iris

Klark Kent

Wazmo Nariz

Klaus Nomi

Plastic Bertrand

Howard Jones

Grace Jones

Nick Lowe

Lene Lovich

Nina Hagen

Nena

Dyan Diamond

Toyah Willcox

Kim Wilde

Tracey Ullman

Carlene Carter

Kirsty MacColl

Pat Benatar

Willy "Loco" Alexander and the Boom Boom Band

Ian Dury and the Blockheads

Graham Parker and the Rumour

Paul Kelly and the Dots

Pearl Harbor and the Explosions

Bruce Wooley and the Camera Club

Jules and The Polar Bears

XTC

Ebn Ozn

Gary Numan

Tubeway Army

Fun Boy Three

Holly and the Italians

Men At Work

Men Without Hats

Missing Persons

Simple Minds

Nervus Rex

Culture Club

The Orchids

The Cichlids

The Nuns

Magazine

Cowboys International

The Buggles

Romeo Void

Ultravox

The Swans

The Wild Swans

The Units

The Dickies

Chrome Dinette

The Ruts

The Skids

The Undertones

The Overtones

The Rings

The Rave

The Raves

The Photos

The Phones

Telephone

The Colors

The Colorfield

The Reds

The Red Rockers

The Raybeats

Beat Rodeo

Bugs Tomorrow

The Chords

The Circles

The Shapes

The Sizes

The Kind

Skafish

Tommy Tutone

The Sports

Gruppo Sportivo

Joey Harris and
the Speedsters

Get Wet

Go West

20/20

The Smithereens

The Del Fuegos

The Heat

The Heats

The Heaters

The Innocents

The Freshies

The Cretones
The Rotters
Polyrock
The Eurythmics
The Comateens
The Scooters
The Lambrettas
The Cortinas
The Members

The Adventures
The Look
Novo Combo
Any Trouble
The Pleasers
The Boize
The Neighborhoods
Suburban Lawns
Rachel Sweet &
The Records
Mickey Jupp &
The Cable Layers

Gary Myrick &
the Figures
Billy Karloff &
the Extreme
The Direct Hits
Berlin
Dead Or Alive
Spandau Ballet
Haysi Fantayzee
Scritti Politti
The Teardrop Explodes
Paul Warren and Explorer
Deaf School

The Clocks
Joe "King" Carrasco
and the Crowns
The Dwight
Twilley Band
The Durocs
The Dugites
The Elektrics
The Fools
The Boyfriends
The Nerves
The Last Ones

Named in Japan!

Let's happy making music joy! Rock! Roll! Others! Also! Plus all new today generation of tomorrow! Making many fresh funky way of now! Band Rock People Have Noise Loud Time of Harajuku Parking And Shopping Street And All For World! Hearing Largest Sound! All To Gather From Where Ever! For Ever! How Ever! What Ever! Invent Emo Band Name Before Any One First!

Flap-Noize

Lick Back

B-Monkey

Fat Smell

Sun Batic

Glass Hoppa

Anti-No

Voyage of Afro

Chop Stick

Bouncily Boys

No Smokin'

Milk Robber

Mini Breast

Good Job!!!

A World Shaking Discovery

Special Crew

Real Ability

Afroism

Electric Trouble

Bound Stoppers

Bathtub Shitter

Louddass

Liberated Stain

Tacos Weezer

Bad Attack

Pull & Ass

Thank Anal

Tribal Chair

Fuzzass

54 Nude Honeys

Nitro Man Lunchers

Boowy

Unbone Baby

The Pillows

The Tigers

The Mops

The Roosters

The Boredoms

The Plastics

The Brilliant Green

The Captains

The Bunnys

The Back Horn

The Freshmen

The High-Lows

The Boom

The Golden Cups

The Pees

Groovy Grass

Scuttle Tiara

N-Trance Fish

Team Ohhh

New Black-ism Booty Man

Stance Punks

Bonkin' Clapper

Asian Kung-Fu Generation

Sons of All Pussys

The Buggy Hold Jive's

The Circulators

The Clanvery Mello Jam

Dumpy Macho Wife

By-Sexual

Funk Bear System

Strong Pasta

Shilfee and Tulipcorobockles ××

Jitterin' Jinn

The System of Alive

Core The Child

Shenky Guns

LSD March

The Mad Capsule Markets

One Ok Rock ☺

The Portugal Japan

Tokyo Ska Paradise Orchestra

Doping Panda

The Rodeo Carburetor

The Neat Beats

Zeppet Store

Genious

Lunkhead

Jamaican Cheek

Garlic Boys

Kannivalism

Monkeys Foot Point

Blues Creation

Mummy The Peepshow

Ole Dick Foggy

Janne Da Arc

Maximum The Hormone

Green Milk From The Planet Orange

Special Others

Tokyo Yankees

High and Mighty Color

The Gerogerigegege

Mix Speakers, Inc.

Home Made Kazoku

Blankey Jet City

HUSKING BEE

GODZILLA &
YELLOW GYPSY

RICE

C-UTE

JUSTIN HEATHCLIFF
ACID MOTHERS
TEMPLE

MALICE MIZER

BASEBALL
BEAR

SPREAD
BEAVER
BUMP OF
CHICKEN
FUNKY MONKEY
BABIES

Head Phones President

Buck-Tick

Guitar Vader

Southern All Stars

Blam Honey

Guitar Wolf

Slick And The Busters

Jackie & The Cedrics

Golf & Mike

Smoke Heads

The Snake Core Guy

Thee Michelle Gun Elephant

Snath Control

Yellow Machinegun

We Acediasts

Strong Pasta

W-inds

Show Ya

Super Bad Dude

The Seeker

World's End Girlfriend

The Yellow Monkey

The Version Nuggets

The Chewinggum Weekend

The Zoobombs

The Salinger

Fairy Fore

Die in Cries ☺

Kiiiiiii

Penpals

Shrinp Wark

The Candy Spooky Theater

Flower Travelin' Band

Sambo Master

Sex Machineguns

Papaya Paranoia

Mr. Children

Noodles

Glay ☹

THE ELL WORD

What is the secret? What is the special power? And who dares make the fateful decision between one "L" or two? There's no telling precisely what the hell the mellifluous, bell-pealing, irresistible appeal of a band name that includes some spelling of the sound *ell* in it is, but . . . well, hell, there you go.

One prominent theory suggests that during the 1950s, the makers of Prell shampoo purchased so much TV, radio, print, and billboard advertising that the syllable powerfully imprinted itself on millions of smooth, soft, shiny impressionable teenage brains, entirely shifting the course of Western Civilization and making it much more manageable.

Another scholarly school has suggested that the Ell-Factor takes our Anglo-Saxon-Teutonic tongue tones and sort of Hispanicizes 'em up. As in the difference between a band called, say, the Vikings, and another one called the Del-Vikings. See? Olé! Orale! Of course, you could name your band the El Vikings but that wouldn't make any sense, now would it?

In any case, certain sexy syllables—"ell" most prominent among them— seem to show up again and again in band names and songs, just as do the names of cars (mainly Chevrolets, for some reason) and birds and jet-powered rocket-like things. And clothes. And flowers. And insects and other stuff. Like soap. And shampoo.

●

The Standells	**A9**
The Spandells	
The Shirelles (formerly The Poquellos)	**A10**

●

B1 The Marcels

The Montells

B2 The Myrtells

B3 The Dovells

The Dynels

B4 The Donnels

B5 The Castels

The Castells

B6 The Chanels

B7 The Chantels

The Chantelles

B8 The Chantrells

B9 The Charmels (later The Dixiebelles)

The Caravelles

B10 The Liberty Belles

The Mission Belles

The Belle Stars — C1

The Belles — C2

The Bells

Lindy and the Lavelles — C3

Debbie and the Darnells — C4

The Del Capris

The Deltairs — C5

The Delgatos — C6

The Delgados

The Del-Rhythmettes — C7

The Randells — C8

The Ran-Dells

The Rondells — C9

The Hondells — C10

D1 The Vondells

The Vandals

D2 The Romans

D3 The Trojans

The Barbarians

D4 The Shondells (later Tommy James and the Shondells, then Hog Heaven)

D5 The Dells (formerly the El-Rays)

The Delphonics

D6 The Delphis

D7 The Del-Phis

The Del-Vikings

D8 The Del Rays

D9 The Deltones

Dick Dale and the Del-Tones

D10

TWO TONES BEYOND:
THE AMAZING SKASMONAUTS

I was in the southernmost city in the ass end of New Zealand's most southern island in about 1990 when it all came clear to me. There was a lamppost with a band flyer on it, and from like twenty or thirty or forty yards away, you could see that a black-and-white checkerboard two-tone ska band had a gig somewhere. It was the international signal for ska band. If bluegrass, say, had such clear cut visual signifiers, there'd be bluegrass bands in places like Japan and Italy right now. Oh . . . right—never mind.

THE SKATALITES

THE MAYTALS

THE PARAGONS

THE PIONEERS

THE BEES

THE TERMITES

THE GLADIATORS

THE JAMAICANS

THE ETHIOPIANS

BYRON LEE AND THE DRAGONAIRES

JUSTIN HINDS AND THE DOMINOES

THE MELLO TONES

THE SILVERTONES

THE DYNATONES

THE HEPTONES

THE MELODIANS

THE SUPERSONICS

THE SOUL VENDORS

THE PARTISANS

THE UNBREAKABLE TEA SET

THE SOUL SOUND

THE THREE TOPS

TYRONE AND THE SLICKERS

THE GAYLADS

THE CLARENDONIANS

THE MERRYMEN

THE RULERS

LORD COMIC & HIS COWBOYS

THE VIPS

THE WAILERS

THE SPECIALS

MADNESS

THE BEAT
(The English Beat in the U.S.)

THE SELECTOR

BAD MANNERS

BALD GUYS IN BOWTIES

BAND GEEK MAFIA

THE BOTTLE ROCKET KINGS

CHARLIE AND THE TRUMPET FACTORY

THE CHIP-PUNX

RUDE BUDDHA

RUDER THAN YOU

THE RUDIMENTS

FIVE FINGER DISCOUNT

FIVE IRON FRENZY

FIVE KNUCKLE SHUFFLE

FIVE QUID SHORT

THE GHOUL TONES

THE HALF TONES

THE TINY TONES

THE TOUCH TONES

THE DIALTONES

THE DIABLOTONES

THE DECAPITONES

THE DEBONAIRES

THE NO TONES

NO DOUBT

NO VALUE

NO BARE FEET

NO RESPECT

NO NONSENSE

NOFX

NO ON 15

NOSELESS NIXON

THE OI SCOUTS

SECRET CAJUN BAND

THE GO-NUTS

DON'T KNOW JACK

GOLDFISH DON'T BOUNCE

DOUBLE-O-SEVEN

DOUBLE-O-ZERO

DOUBLE-O-SOMETHING

EVIL TWIN SKIPPY

ATTABOY SKIP

THE GOPS

LET'S GO BOWLING

SUPERBALL

THE SUPERVILLAINS

THE SUPER PINEAPPLES

PORK PIE TRIBE

THE PIETASTERS

PROFESSOR PLUM

RECESS REJECTS

THE SKANKIN' PICKLES

SKANK LIKE FRANK

THE REVERBTONES

THE RASCAL KINGS

THE ROYAL NOISE BRIGADE

THE ROYAL RANGERS

THE ROYALTIES

THE SCATOLOGISTS

THE ALCOSKALICS

THE DECEPTICONZ

THE SHRINERS OF SKA

SKA TREK

SKAHUMBUG

THE SKABURBIANS

THE SKADOLESCENTS

THE SKAKABOBS

SKA'D FOR LIFE

SKA CAPELLA

SKABBA THE HUT

THE SKALAPENOS

THE SKALETT LETTER

SKALI BABA AND THE
FORTY OUNCE HORNS

SKALIOSIS

THE SKAM

THE SKAMIGOS

SKAMAKAZE

THE SKAMATICS

THE SKAMADORES

THE SKAMPS

204

THE SKANDALS

SKA FACE

THE SKATAPULTS

THE SKADILLACS

SKAGINA

SKAMUNISTS

SKANDANAVIA

SKAPONE

SKARRED BY SKA

THE SKASTAFARIANS

SKATLAND YARD

SKAFACE

SKASQUATCH

SKATURDAY

SKAZILLA

SKATET

THE SKAFLAWS

THE SKAMETS

THE SKATTERBRAINS

THE SKAUTHENTICS

THE SKAVACADOS

SKAVENJAH

THE SKAWALKERS

SKAZEL TOV!

THE SKELETONES

THE SLOPPY POPSICLES

THE SPACE SKADETS

THE SPITVALVES

THE STRAIGHT EDGE
CRACK WHORES

THE TINY TONES

THE TOUCH TONES

THE TOASTERS

TOKYO SKA PARADISE
ORCHESTRA

THE TRITONES

THE TWISTOFFS

THE COVER GIRLS

URINAL MINT

LATEX PENGUIN

THE FURIOUS TURTLES

THE LEMON MERCHANTS

THE TROJAN HORNS

ARMY OF JUAN

FLUXSKAPACITOR

FREE CHEESE FOR ALL
(Switzerland)

CATCH 22

THE IMPERIALS

THE SKALARS

THE JAVATONES

THE TONES

THE UPTONES

LEE HARVEY SKASWALD

JOHNNY UNITE US

Punk Names

Now, like I said elsewhere, it's absolutely necessary, it's mandatory, that you make up your own punk name. If your tattooed, nose-ringed, Roller Derbyin', PTA-leadin' mom names you Charlie Monoxide, that's lame. L-A-M-E, with an O. It's pathetic. It's sad, and entirely inappropriate. And just that the other little dears named Johnny Rotten on account of his dental hygiene hijinks doesn't disprove my point at all. Because it's perfectly OK if your own little gang of Ramones all declare yourselves Johnny, and Mikey, and Cassius, and Louis-Louis Scabpicker, of the soon-to-be locally famous the Scabpickers, brothers in blood if not actual blood-brothers. It's just that for Louis-Louis Scabpicker to be your actual punk name, the one that sticks for life, basically like a tattoo you can't afford to remove, well, it's got to be even more ridiculously revelatory about your inner supervillain than the truly awesome band name you picked earlier that same rehearsal. So just be sure you aren't actually MC Louis-Louis King Scabpicker instead.

Johnny Rotten

Sid Vicious

Rat Scabies

Captain Sensible

Joe Strummer

Tory Crimes

Wreckless Eric

Billy Idol

Jello Biafra

Jello B. Afro

Poly Styrene

Richard Hell

Johnny Thunders

Steve Ignorant

Elton Motello

Adam Ant

Elvis Costello

Billy Bragg

Sting

Nikki Sudden

Richard Strange

Mink DeVille

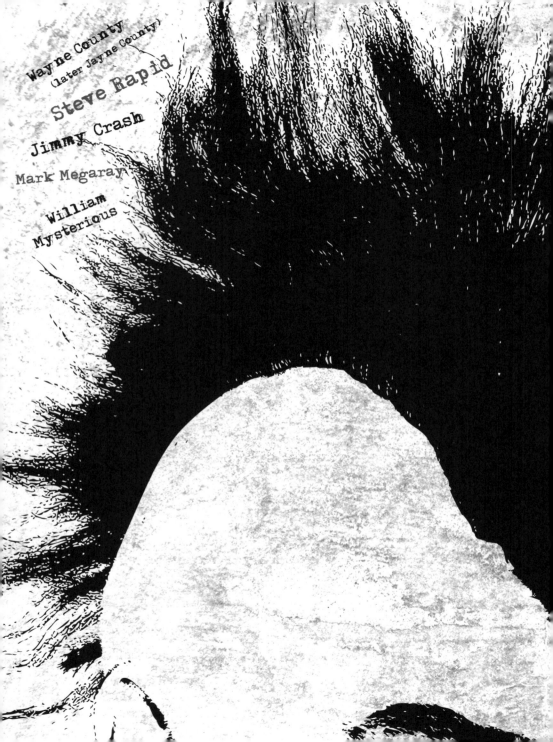

Wayne County
(later Jayne County)

Steve Rapid

Jimmy Crash

Mark Megaray

William
Mysterious

Gail Warning

Johnny Terminator   Dee Generate   Ari Up

Simon Templar   Jah Wobble

Tomata du Plenty

John Doe   Palmolive

Robert Gotobed

Billy Zoom   Darby Crash
(previously Bobby Pyn)

Exene

Nick Knox   Alice Bag

Pat Bag

Nicky Beat

Darren Peligro

Stiv Bators   Nicky Tesco

Johnny Blitz   Joey Ramone

Cheetah Chrome   Johnny Ramone

—Jeff Magnum   Dee Dee Ramone
(later, briefly, MCDD)

Jimmy Zero   Tommy Ramone

Marky Ramone

Johnny Moped   Connie Ramone
Handsome Dick Manitoba

Gaye Advert

Dick Valentine

Sue Catwoman
Kim O Therapy

Brian Damage   Mike Modern   Bill Bored

Bruce Loose   Frank Discussion

Will Shatter
Lee Ving
Derf Scratch
Spit Stix
Geza X
Rob Graves
Dinah Cancer
Pat Smear
Joey Shithead
Rock Vodka
Smog Vomit
Texacala Jones
Cheetah Chrome
Stiv Bators
Johnny Blitz
Jimmy Zero
Jeff Magnum
Crocus Behomoth
Bono Vox
The Edge
Billy Childish
Simon Bob Sinister

Prog!

So, your band, Recombinant Structural Cellularity (previously known as PreMacro Quintessence), unquestionably delivers its own completely unique synthesis that transcends genre and label and has its own Wikipedia page listing all current and former members and their musical influences, but you mainly gig on alternating Monday nights, because that's when the Straw Hat Pizza Parlor on Chestnut Avenue has a night devoted to progressive rock (unlike the Wednesday night devoted to jam-band bluegrass where they try to wedge progressive in like it was anchovies on a Canadian Bacon/Pineapple Hawaiian Sicilian Supreme), because the Monday night manager always wanted to be in a band, but suffers from congenital neural amusia, which has proven to be a limiting factor for him, although lately he's learning drums through statistical analysis of fractal patterns. (The band that plays the other alternate Mondays of the month is two acoustic guitar guys who call themselves Keltik UniKorn, and they're really smug about the fact that they have like three girls—one Wiccan, one goth, one undeclared—who regularly come to see them.) Moreover, there's no sound check and you have to be out of there, gear and all, by 11:15 sharp, when they start turning off the ovens.) You put up with the demeaning surroundings because otherwise there would be nowhere else to play but in fact, both you and your keyboard player feel that you are altering the envelope of the entire proto-prog/neo-progressive sub-genre. And yes, all the band members wear glasses, but you wear them onstage because you have to be able to read the sheet music in order to follow the vast number of never-before-assembled chord changes. Your keyboard player has glasses, and your drummer has glasses, and everybody else in the band except the lead singer wears glasses. He has them but doesn't wear them because he doesn't feel he should read chord charts onstage, so it ends up looking like he's the leader of a band full of accountants and Internet geeks. There have been three entire band meetings specifically devoted to this issue, each more unproductive than the last. Your keyboard player has written a program that prints the music in a musical notation of his own invention that he intends to patent. The band's multisyllabic mouthful of a name takes advantage of the fact that both your bass player and your drummer—the drummer, for God's sake—are fluent in Esperanto and Unix. Your band's original logo had a footnote but they kept leaving it out of the local entertainment listings. Imbeciles!

The Soft Machine

Colosseum

Caravan

Gong

Hatfield & the North

Egg

National Health

The Wilde Flowers

Pink Floyd

Khan

Matching Mole

Henry Cow

Van Der Graaf Generator

Gentle Giant

Quiet Sun

Supersister

Rush

Premiata Forneria Marconi (PFM)

Banco Del Mutuo Soccorso

Rovescio Della Medaglia (RDM)

Gryphon

Renaissance

SBB

Can

Popul Vuh

Guru Guru

Faust

Neu!

Ash Ra Tempel

Amon Düül

Kraftwerk

Tangerine Dream

Heldon

Lard Free

Shakti

Godspeed You Black
Emperor

Sigur Ros

A Silver Mt. Zion

Tortoise

Mogwai

Ulver

Lazona

Santana

Return to Forever

Mahavishnu Orchestra

Billy Cobham's Spectrum

The Tony Williams Lifetime

Weather Report

Larry Coryell's
Eleventh House

Stomu Yamashta's Go

Passport

Hawkwind

Nektar

Ozric Tentacles

Marillion

Quintessence

Third Ear Band

Wishbone Ash

Genesis

The Rambling Playboy Brothers

Maybe it's being raised on a farm. Because people actually used to be raised on farms. Not like chickens or cows—it was the people who actually raised the chickens and cows and stuff—but once upon a time, not so long ago, human beings were often born and raised and lived and died on farms. I swear to God!

Well, apparently, when these farmboys got around to putting 'em together a band, they pretty much always called it something that had either "Ramblers" or "Playboys" in the name. Because they probably weren't much of either one, but they were a lot more of both than the people who came to see 'em. The Brother part I shouldn't have to explain, unless you were born in a damn barn or something.

216

Bob Wills and The Texas Playboys

Bill Woods' Orange Blossom Playboys

Steve Riley and the Mamou Playboys

Kevin Naquin and the Ossun Playboys

The Big Town Playboys

The Gulf Coast Playboys

Wynn Stewart's West Coast Playboys

The San Diego Cajun Playboys

The Honolulu Playboys

Jimmie Revard and the Oklahoma Playboys

Rosie Ledet and the Zydeco Playboys

Gary Lewis and the Playboys

The Thousand Dollar Playboys

John Fred and His Playboy Band

The Faux Playboys

Aldus Roger and the Lafayette Playboys

The Intercontinetal Playboys

Scottie Pousson and the Pointe
Aux Loups Playboys

The Latin Playboys

The Chicago Playboys

Thelma Terry and Her Playboys

JB and the Playboys

The Belmont Playboys

The Gadjo Playboys

The Moonshine Playboys

The Sundown Playboys

The Mystic Playboys

The Space Age Playboys

The Cachagua Playboys

John O'Hara and the Playboys

The Balkan Playboys

The Mountain Playboys

Terrence Simen & the Mallet Playboys

Banjo Dan and the Mid-Nite Plowboys

The Psychic Plowboys

The New Lost City Ramblers

The Rockin' Plowboys

The Red Stick Ramblers

The Red Clay Ramblers

The Hackberry Ramblers

The Tarbox Ramblers

The Dublin City Ramblers

    The Modena City Ramblers

The Rincon Ramblers

    The Reckless Ramblers

The Hogwaller Ramblers

    The Midnight Ramblers
    (Rolling Stones tribute band
    from Stavanger, Norway)

The Midnight Ramblers
(the University of Rochester
all-male a cappella chorus)

    The Lost Bayou Ramblers

The Acadian Ramblers

    The Rockhouse Ramblers

The Riverboat Ramblers

    The Courthouse Ramblers

The Pine Hill Ramblers

    The California Ramblers

Ramblers Traditional Jazz
Band de Brasil

Ramblers Dansmusik Orkester

    Delta Ramblers
    (Orange County, CA)

Hazel and the Delta Ramblers
(New Orleans, LA)

    Lonesome Road Ramblers

Skegness Ramblers

    Jesse Lege and the
    Southern Ramblers

The Steel City Ramblers

    Laurel Canyon Ramblers

Charlie Poole and His
North Carolina Ramblers

    Roy Harvey and the North
    Carolina Ramblers

Allen Thibidoux and the
French Ramblers

    The Dixie Ramblers

The Nash Ramblers

    The Chemical Brothers

The Allman Brothers

The Righteous Brothers

    The Chambers Brothers

The Mills Brothers

    The Cornelius Brothers
and Sister Rose

The Maddox Brothers
and Sister Rose

    The Doobie Brothers

The Ringling Sisters

    The Blues Brothers

The Louvin Brothers

    The Brothers Four

The Bacon Brothers

    The Monroe Brothers

The Stanley Brothers

    The Osbourne Brothers

The Everly Brothers

    The Delmore Brothers

The Blue Sky Boys
(the Bolick Brothers)

The Funk Brothers

    The Campbell Brothers

The Brothers Gibb

    The Osmond Brothers

The Warren Brothers

    The Holmes Brothers

The Gatlin Brothers

    Five Chinese Brothers

The Isley Brothers

    The Flying Burrito Brothers

The Flying Other Brothers

    The Clancy Brothers and
Tommy Makem

The Blackfoot Brothers

    The Waco Brothers

The Walker Brothers

    The Statler Brothers

The Smothers Brothers

    The Collins Kids

Headbanger's All

The history of heavy metal is wreathed in clouds of mystery pouring confusion on the ground. Either Motörhead or Blue Öyster Cult invented the umlaut; Ronnie James Dio's Italian grandmother invented the Hail-Satan-Hook-'Em-Horns hand gesture; Jimi Hendrix invented the fuzzbox and the wah-wah pedal, and the Marshall stack and the Stratocaster, so that Eddie Van Halen could invent fretboard tapping; Yngwie Malmsteen invented the Mixolydian scale, mainly so he wouldn't have to sound like Jimi Hendrix; Black Sabbath invented having the name of the band, and the name of the first album, and the name of the first song on the first album all be the same thing. Ozzy invented biting the heads off bats and doves, and Alice Cooper invented killing chickens and carrying snakes. Iron Maiden invented sleeveless denim jackets, and Judas Priest's Rob Halford invented butt-less leather chaps, and Robert Plant invented bell-bottoms, while Jimmy Page invented the guitar with two necks, and nobody really cares who invented the one with three. KISS invented merchandise and Polaroids, and Ginger Baker invented the double kick drum set, while Def Leppard invented the one-armed drummer. Slayer invented speed metal and Metallica invented Napster.

But the really great thing is that none of them thought to put a patent or a copyright on any of it, so you can basically snag any of it, slap an umlaut on it, and call it your own. Or two umlauts, for emphasis and effect.

Blue Cheer	Winger
Iron Butterfly	Bon Jovi
Love Sculpture	Kix
Mountain	Poison
Hawkwind	Jackyl
Black Sabbath	Megadeth
Deep Purple	Warrant
Led Zeppelin	White Lion
Blue Öyster Cult	Whitesnake
KISS	Dokken
Motörhead	Cinderella
The Scorpions	Tesla
Judas Priest	Europe
Iron Maiden	Slaughter
Saxon	Stryper
Def Leppard	Skid Row
Metallica	Warlock
Quiet Riot	Manowar
Mötley Crüe	Armored Saint
Ratt	Faith No More

Jane's Addiction

Venom

Anthrax

Suicidal Tendencies

Nine Inch Nails

Alice In Chains

Rage Against
The Machine

Testament

Slayer

Overkill

Death

Danzig

Celtic Frost

Treponem Pal

Mercyful Fate

Loudness

GWAR

W.A.S.P.

Fates Warning

Accept

Anvil

Armored Saint

Cannibal Corpse

Dangerous Toys

Cessation of Life

D.A.D. (previously
Disneyland After
Dark [litigation])

Queensrÿche

Danger Danger

Pretty Boy Floyd

Hans Naughty

Denied Existence

Destroy

Destruction

Dying Fetus

Dying Sun

Dead

Death

Death Angel	Funeral
Death Row	Dark Funeral
Death Wish	Old Funeral
Fastway	Dismal Euphony
Faster Pussycat	Dream Death
Angry Clown	Dream Evil
Chaotic Realm	UFO
Great White	Angel Witch
Depression	Diamond Head
Destiny's End	Venom
Hellion	Cryptic Slaugher
Kreator	Kreator
Demon	Prong
Demon Realm	Corrosion of Conformity
Kingdom Come	Destruction
Lääz Rockit	Bathory
Flotsam and Jetsam	Sodom
Morbid	Hellhammer
Enuff Z'nuff	Sepultura
Dark Angel	

Possessed	Kong
Carcass	DESTRÖYER 666
Godflesh	Cradle of Filth
Necrovore	Immortal
Morbid Angel	Immolation
Massacra	Imprecation
Hypocrisy	Incantation
Vader	Enslaved
Morpheus	Cadaver
Sinister	Mutilation
Suffocaton	Acerbus
Cryptopsy	At the Gates
Demigod	Defleshed
Defiance	Deeds of Flesh
Dementia	Gutted
Monstrosity	Kataklysm
Deicide	Pyrexia
Unleashed	Chronical Diarrhoea
Atheist	Abomination
Cynic	Adramelech

Amorphis
Ancient Rites
Asphyx
Cenotaph
Centinex
Massacre
Molested
Monstrosity
Ceremony
Deathstrike
Deceased
Entombed
Flesherawl
God Macabre
Mortuary
Mythic
Gorguts
Grotesque
Atrocity

Autopsy
Baphomet
Cadaver
Cartilage
Hetsheads
Hypocrisy Infester
Kilcrops
Detritus
Diabolical
Masquerade
Lepra
Grotesque
Havohej
Hades
Ildjarn
Magus
Summoning
Thorns
Varathron
Morpheus Descends

Necromass	Deteriorate
Necrophiliac	Dismember
Necrophobic	Behemoth
Nuclear Death	Blasphemy
Num Skull	Eucharist
Obituary	Gehenna
Rise	Burzum
Revenant	Dissection
Sadistic Intent	Emperor
Seance	Gorgoroth
Sentenced	Graveland
Thanatopsis	Ceremonium
Therion	Ceremony
Torchure	Deeds of Flesh
Belial	Hate Eternal
Unanimated	Intestine Baalism
Uncanny	Impaled Nazarene
Unleashed	Marduk
Bathory	Mayhem
Demilich	Merciless

Dark Half	Capharnaum
Darkmoon	Luciferion
Dark Moor	Mortem
Dark Throne	Oppressor
Dark Tranquility	Pessimist
Profanatica	Rise
Rotting Christ	Abruptum
Mütiilation	Absurd
Mysticum	The Abyss
Necromantia	Ancient
Sacramentum	Angelcorpse
Samael	Antaeus
Sarcofago	Arcturus
Septic Flesh	Auzhia
Oppressor	Avenger
Pessimist	Black Goat
Pestilence	Vilkates
Von	Watain
Zyklon-B	Cultus Sanguine
Asgard	Dark Tranquility

Dawn	Niden Div 187
Deinonychius	NME
Demonic	Ophthalamia
Demoncy	Pentagram
Dissection	Pervertum
Frozen Shadows	Sammath
Blasphemy	Septic Flesh
Blazemth	Setherial
Blood	Swordmaster
Gotmoor	Tartaros
Infernum	Throne of Ahaz
Inquisition	Ulver
Resuscitator	Ungod
I Shalt Become	Xibalba
Kvist	Yamatu
Urgrund	White Skull
Usurper	Steel Prophet
Lord Wind	Sacred Steel
Manes	Biomechanical
Mortiis	Balistik Kick

Grim Reaper	Deliverance
Iron Savior	Helloween
Malice	Napalm
Metal Church	Napalm Death
Nocturnal Rites	Onslaught
Rage	Godflesh
Savatage	Godhead
Acid Reign	Malignant Eternal
Annhiliator	Misery Loves Co.
Anvil Bitch	Puncture
Blood Feast	Bang Tango
Carnal Forge	Bangkok Shock
Sorcier des Glaces	Bitch
Summon	Alcatrazz
Summoning	Britny Fox
Dearly Beheaded	BulletBoyz
Demolition Hammer	Cinderella
Destruction	Coverdale/Page
Destructor	Krokus
Detante	LA Guns

Scorpions	Smashed Gladys
Lynch Mob	Skid Row
Kingdom Come	Shotgun Messiah
Black n' Blue	Saigon Kick
London	Hanoi Rocks
Love/Hate	Rock City Angels
Damn Yankees	King Diamond
Danger Danger	Katatonia
Dirty Blonde	Krieg
Junkyard	Dio
Jetboy	Ritual Carnage
Y&T	Vengeance Rising
XYZ	Voice of Destruction
Vyper	Sacred Reich
Vinnie Vincent Invasion	Sacrilege B.C.
Tuff	Rigor Mortis
Trixter	Powermad
Tora Tora	Overkill

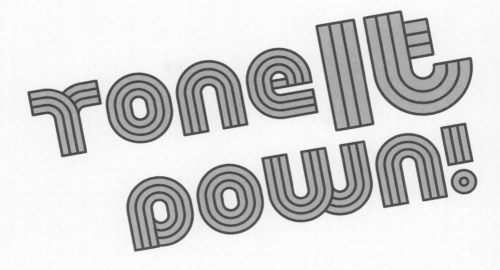

When it comes to band names, of course, we're dealing purely in fashion, in mystery and magic and metaphysics, in arcane alchemical formulae. (Especially, as to that last one—if you're a prog-rock band planning a rock-opera trilogy or two, you can pretty much build it by shifting those three words around to name either the albums or the band, but preferably not both.) Certain sibilant syllables pack powerful punches. For a decade or so, for instance, just adding "tones" to the end of your band's name miraculously adds a power, a glory, a majesty that just can't be denied. And that "n" sound. So smooth, so young, so nubile, so teen. And then, out of the blue, that power disappears, vanishes, evaporates, makes you look like a bunch of dopey-ass cornball losers. Which accounts for the absence of bands named the Beatletones, the Spice Girl–tones, the U2tones, the White Stripe–tones, and . . . And You Will Know Us By The Trail Of Dead Tones.

The Crewd

The Tones

The Bob Crewe
Generation

The Tonettes

The Tren-Teens

The Deb-Tones

The Velveteens

The Delltones

The Velvet-teens

The Monotones

The Teen Kings

The Quintones

The Teenage Kings
of Harmony

The Joytones

Johnny and
the Velvetones

The Teen Queens

The Royal Teens

Tony and the
Tonebenders

The Del Tones

Tony Toni Toné

Dick Dale and
the Del-Tones

The Mighty Mighty
Bosstones

The Teentones

The Short Cuts

The Six Teens

The Crew Cuts

The Mello Tones

The Crew

The Tempo Tones

The Three Teens

The Threeteens

The Linc-Tones

The Tiny Tones

The Clef-Tones

The Touch Tones

The Spongetones

The Tube Tones

The Pain Teens

The Reverbtones

The Coma-Teens

The Dialtones

The Nashville Teens

The Diablotones

Shane Fenton and the Fentones

The Pendletones

The Temptones
(later Hall & Oates)

The TikiTones

The Madtones

Evelyn Dell and the Vibratones

The Clamtones

The Undertones

The Debonaires

The Ghoul Tones

The Teen Bugs

The Half Tones

The Teentones

The Wet-Tones

The Chaperones

The Decapitones

The Tone

Blues Names

So the deal with blues names is you can go ahead and give yourself one, but you do so at great risk; it has all been tried and attempted before. For example, Sonny Boy is not the sort of name you'd give yourself, nowadays anyway, to show what a blood-spittin' bluesman you are, but the original Sonny Boy Williamson was so righteous and cool that, well, Sonny Boy Williamson Number Two just flat out stole and took his name. And whether because of time and circumstances, or because Sonny Boy Williamson was too powerful a name for merely one man, or because of the looseness of copyright laws when you don't have a lawyer to enforce 'em, or, well, hell, just because . . . the Sonny Boy Williamson we know today is the one we call Sonny Boy Williamson II. And if we know the other one, the original one, it's because we've vaguely heard there used to be an original Sonny Boy Williamson. There's a lesson in there somewhere, but it beats me what it is.

John Lee Hooker (aka John Lee Cooker, John Lee Booker, John Lee, Texas Slim, Birmingham Sam and His Magic Guitar, Delta John, The Boogie Man, Johnny Lee, Johnny Williams, Little Pork Chops, John L. Booker, Sir John Lee Hooker, others)

Muddy Waters

Howlin' Wolf

Lightnin' Hopkins

Son House

Magic Sam

Little Walter

Big Walter Horton

Big Bill Broonzy

Big Crawford

Otis Spann

Pinetop Perkins

Pine Top Smith

Ramblin' Henry Thomas

Papa Charlie Jackson

Brother Willie Eason

B. B. King

Albert King

Freddie King

Little Freddie King

Earl Hooker

Tommy Johnson

Lonnie Johnson

Robert Johnson

Robert Jr. Lockwood

Johnny Shines

Little Junior Parker

Li'l Son Jackson

Little Brother Montgomery

Koko Taylor

Bobby "Blue" Bland

Big Mama Thornton

Big Maceo

Big Joe McCoy

Blind Lemon Jefferson

Bumble Bee Slim

Memphis Minnie

Sister Rosetta Tharpe

Arizona Dranes

T-Bone Walker

Sonny Boy Williamson
(Number One and Number Two)

Ma Rainey

Bessie Smith

Blue Lu Barker

Blind Willie Johnson

Blind Lemon Jefferson

Blind Willie McTell

Cryin' Sam Collins

Blind Blake	Big Boy Cleveland
Blind Boy Fuller	Montana Taylor
Blind Teddy Darby	Reverend Robert Wilkins
Blind Joe Taggert	Reverend Blind Gary Davis
Blind Arvella Graves	Reverend Lonnie Farris
Blind Roosevelt Graves	Reverend Al Green
Black Ace	Governor Jimmie Davis
The Grey Ghost	Doctor Clayton
Barbecue Bob	Doctor Ross
Clarence "Gatemouth" Brown	Professor Longhair
Clarence "Bon Ton" Garlow	Elder Charles Beck
Cripple Clarence Lofton	Oscar Woods
Champion Jack Dupree	Rabbit Brown
Cow Cow Davenport	Charley Patton
Speckled Red	Hambone Willie Newbern
Tampa Red	James "Boodle It" Wiggins
Piano Red	Kingfish Bill Tomlin
Georgia Tom	Butterbeans & Susie
St. Louis Jimmy Oden	Jaybird Coleman
St. Louis Bessie	Sonny Rhodes
Memphis Slim	Big Road Webster Parker
Kokomo Arnold	Uncle Bud Walker

238

Geechie Wiley	Slim Harpo
Pee Wee Crayton	Jazz Gillum
Amos Milburn	Washboard Sam
Charlie "Bozo" Nickerson	J. B. Hutto and the Hawks
Furry Lewis	Louis Jordan and His Tympany Five
Little Hat Jones	Peetie Wheatstraw
Bobbie Cadillac	Jimmy Witherspoon
Pink Anderson	Bo Diddley
Floyd "Dipper Boy" Council	Chuck Berry
Mance Lipscomb	Lead Belly (Huddie Ledbetter)
Whistlin' Alex Moore	Percy Mayfield
Kid Prince Moore	Mississippi John Hurt
Prince Albert Hunt	Mississippi Fred McDowell
Prince	Little Milton
Leroy Carr	Clifton Chenier
Robert Nighthawk	Bukka (Booker) White
Roosevelt Sykes	Sleepy John Estes
Big Joe Williams	Skip James
Big Joe Turner	Johnny Shines
Arthur "Big Boy" Crudup	Wynonie Harris
Hound Dog Taylor	David "Honeyboy" Evans

Brownie McGhee	Jimmy McCracklin
Sonny Terry	Junior Kimbrough
Scrapper Blackwell	R. L. Burnside
Junior Wells	T Model Ford
Doctor Ross	Son Seals
Sunnyland Slim	James "Super Chikan" Johnson
Bill Doggett	Z. Z. Hill
Guitar Slim	Little Johnny Taylor
Guitar Gable	Sugar Pie DeSanto
Johnny "Guitar" Watson	Etta James
Jessie Mae Hemphill	Ike Turner
Jazz Gillum	Paul Butterfield
One String Sam	Mike Bloomfield
Ironing Board Sam	Elvin Bishop
Smokey Hogg	Charlie Musselwhite
Lowell Fulson	Tony "Little Sun" Glover
Funny Paper Smith	Al "Blind Owl" Wilson
Kansas City Kitty	Bob "Bear" Hite
KC Douglas	Henry "Sunflower" Vestine
Freddie Roulette	Harvey "The Snake" Mandel
L. C. "Good Rockin'" Robinson	Barry Goldberg

The Decadent Decline of the Psychedelic Nomenclatures, or the Exploding Plastic Inevitable

Somewhere in here, somewhere between the Lemon Pipers and the Doodletown Pipers, between Underground Sunshine and Up With People, between the Peppermint Rainbow and the Peanut Butter Conspiracy, a nagging suspicion begins to rise. Despite their matching orange and purple Nehru jackets, despite their super-groovy striped bell-bottoms and super-wide mod belts, it's entirely possible that none of these people have ever actually tasted any LSD-25. They may be fakin' it.

Underground Sunshine

The Electric Prunes

The Spiral Staircase

The Neon Philharmonic

The Original Caste

The Flying Machine

The Peppermint Rainbow

John Lennon and the Plastic Ono Band

Dick Hyman and His Electric Eclectics

Enoch Light and The Brass Menagerie

The 1910 Fruitgum Company

Professor Morrison's Lollipop

Edison Lighthouse

The Peanut Butter Conspiracy

The Popcorn Blizzard

Lt. Garcia's Magic Music Box

The Waterproof Tinkertoy

Up With People

The Doodletown Pipers

The Sunshine Generation

The National Gallery

The Now Geneneration

The Fifth Dimension

The Assembled Multitude

The Brotherhood of Man

The Mike Curb Congregation

The Bob Crewe Generation

The Marshmellow Steamshovel

The Strawberry Alarm Clock

Stuffy and His Frozen Parachute Band

The Chocolate Watch Band

The Amazing Friendly Apple

The Ball Point Banana

The Conception Corporation

W.C. Fields Memorial Electric String Band

Hamilton, Joe Frank, & Reynolds

The Beginning of the End

The Top 99 or so

Greatest Band Names Ever

Without Question

(in No Particular Order)

Painstaking, state-of-the-art, scientific research conducted in a germ-stabilized laboratory environment have verified the following as unquestionably the finest examples of band-nameology in the History of Western Civilization. No animals were harmed in the process, though several drummers were ritually slaughtered.

ABBA

Shot Down Over Equador Jr.

The Sex Pistols

The Del-Vikings

DEVO

. . . And You Will Know Us by the Trail of Dead

All Girl Summer Fun Band

Hank Williams and The Drifting Cowboys

The Plastic People of the Universe

Black Sabbath

Killing Joke

The Barbarians

Judas Priest

Scritti Politti

The Fendermen

Parliament-Funkadelic

Black Flag

The Bar-Kays

Free Beer

James Brown and the New New Super Heavy James Brown Revue

Richard Hell and The Voidoids

Top Jimmy and
The Rhythm Pigs

Loudness

Reparata and the
Delrons

The Beverly
Hillbillies
(successful litigation
against television show)

Bad Brains

Motörhead

Earth, Wind & Fire

The Circle Jerks

Faith No More

The Guilloteens

The Shadows

of Knight

King Midas and
the Mufflers

Grandmaster Flash
and The Furious Five

Sublime

Corrosion of
Conformity

The Screamin'
Sirens

Buck Owens
& the Buckaroos

The Upsetters
(from New Orleans or
Jamaica, take your pick)

Jelly Roll Morton's
Red Hot Chili
Peppers

Jack Off Jill

Cradle of Filth

The Runaways

X (from Australia, Japan, and Los Angeles, take your pick)

Blue Öyster Cult (mit umlaut)

The Killer Barbies

The Beatles

The Vantours

Bolt Thrower

Buffalo Springfield

Professor Longhair and His Shuffling Hungarians

The Brides of Funkenstein

James Brown and The Famous Flames

The Rhythm Orchids

Sam The Sham and The Pharoahs

Quiet Riot

The Minutemen

Kraftwerk

Armored Saint

Disco Tex and The Sex-O-Lettes

The Sons of the Pioneers

Manic Street Preachers

The Treacherous Three

The Gun Club

Tool

The Teenage Kings of Harmony

Stark Naked and The Car Thieves

I Spit On Your Gravy

Dead Kennedys

Slayer

The Soup Dragons

Built To Spill

Iron Maiden

Brenda and the Tabulations

The Angry Samoans

The Fatback Band

Commander Cody and His Lost Planet Airmen

Nine Inch Nails

The Meat Puppets

Rage Against The Machine

Avenged Sevenfold

The Drifters

Girls Vs. Boys

Bongwater	The Bop Kings
The Pop Group	The New Riders of the Purple Sage
BMX Bandits	The Banana Splits
Martha and the Vandellas	Machine Screw
The Rip Chords	Wormfood
Lords of Acid	The Marvelettes
Dearly Beheaded	Judas Priest
The Turbans	The Sonics
Spooky Tooth	Steppenwolf
Booker T. and the MGs	

"Our band could be your life."

-- The Minutemen